SARAH IVENS

get REAL

Embrace your strengths,
accept your limits and create an
authentically happier, healthier you

PIATKUS

PIATKUS

First published in Great Britain in 2021 by Piatkus

1 3 5 7 9 10 8 6 4 2

A CIP catalogue record for this book
is available from the British Library.

ISBN 978-0-349-42609-9

Typeset in Swift by M Rules
Printed and bound in Great Britain by Clays Ltd, Elcograf S.p.A

Papers used by Piatkus are from well-managed forests
and other responsible sources.

Piatkus
An imprint of
Little, Brown Book Group
Carmelite House
50 Victoria Embankment
London EC4Y 0DZ

An Hachette UK Company
www.hachette.co.uk

www.littlebrown.co.uk

NOTE: the names of individuals have been changed to protect their privacy.

For my god-daughters Georgia Brown, Lola Reynolds and Anna Misata, and niece Isobella Ivens – don't be like the rest of them, dear darlings!

Contents

Acknowledgements

Without friends sharing their most fragile moments and triumphant revelations with me, this book would be so much weaker, and I truly appreciate their honesty. Thanks to the various teachers who have inspired me to look within and trust my gut, instead of craning my neck to worry about the competition or trying to be something I'm not. From my professors and PhD cohort at the University of Louisville, to my various well-being instructors, to the scientists and scholars who share their research, and my agent Tom Miller at Liza Dawson Associates in New York, and my writer-friend-heroes Leah Hampton and Annalisa Barbieri – your wisdom is priceless. The team at Piatkus and Little, Brown are true publishing empaths, working hard to share their love of good writing and great ideas with the world. As Matt Haig said so smartly, 'When anger trawls the internet, looking for a hook; it's time to disconnect and go and read a book.' We've never needed the likes of Jillian Young, Jillian Stewart, Bernadette Marron and Beth Wright et al., more! And lastly, thanks to my husband Russell for occupying the kids so that I could actually get some work done during these discombobulating times. It's nice to hear the three of you laughing at *Fawlty Towers* upstairs while I write – even if you're supposed to be teaching them Spanish.

Acknowledgments

Introduction

'The essence of being human is that
one does not seek perfection.'

George Orwell

Tomorrow will be calmer. This year will be kinder. It has to be, right? Because we're exhausted, aren't we? Whether it's due to the never-ending stream of negative news, a money worry hanging over us, a health concern we've been coping with, or simply the fact that our life is full to the point of bursting, we're feeling fragile. Perhaps your life is just filled with *meh* people, places and plotlines – and you're drifting through it with a lack of enthusiasm, joy or interest.

For many of us, it feels like the goal posts of life keep moving and we're kicking the ball in our own net, losing whatever ability we had to keep our head in the game. Too often, flustered, we stop focusing on our own path and what our next move should be. We're too busy or worried about what everyone else is doing to trust our instincts or believe in our talents ... but we should! Because two of the most important lessons I've learnt in life are that:

1. We do not have to participate in any game that we
    don't want to – a game that feels false, or harmful, or
    stressful.
2. We should safeguard our health and happiness as
    much as anyone else's. We can pick up the ball and
    walk away. We are not only a player in our precious,
    authentic, beautiful life, we are the referee, too.

If you feel like a spectator in your too stressful, too full or
too *meh* life, you need to edit out what isn't working for you.
You need to stop, look, take your foot off the brake ... and think
about what is right for you. I did, and it has been revolutionary.

Since childhood I've been blasted with societal pressures to
strive, thrive, exceed, expect and achieve – and fit in with the
gang. Be more like her. Get involved in everything. Cling on
tight. Climb every mountain. It's only recently that I've owned
the fact that I don't *want* to climb every mountain. In fact, I
might be calmer and more content if I avoided mountains alto-
gether and just took on the few hills that looked appealing. I've
stopped reaching for the unachievable – and even more unmain-
tainable – goal of perfection and edited my life to a workable
point of self-knowledge where I can embrace my strengths and
accept my limits. Doing this has helped me be more, well, *me*
and move towards greater health and happiness.

In order to start *your* new story, you need to become the
editor of your most important work – you. Every new day is a
fresh start, every new year is a chance for renewal, each birthday is a clean page to start writing a new story on. Not a *perfect*
start or story that has to be set in stone but a workable one that
upholds your true values, dreams and goals as you take life at

your own pace, day by day, looking after yourself and those you love. That means getting real about what matters to you and carrying out an 'authenticity edit', because only by being truly honest with yourself can you find the self-acceptance, self-compassion and self-belief to embrace your strengths and accept your limits. This will involve carefully reconsidering your purpose, your goals, your relationships, your self-care and your ability to change and let things go. An authenticity edit will allow you to identify what you want more *or* less of in your life, who you need more *or* less of in your social circle, and the mental health tools *and* physical health changes that will benefit you most. It will remind you that it is your choice whether you say yes or no, speed up or slow down, engage with your extroverted or introverted side. Not a made-up version of perfect you; the real you. And this is what you'll learn how to do, along with many more self-healing techniques, over the following nine chapters of *Get Real*.

What does it mean to get real and be authentically, uniquely you? It means to be self-aware, to be secure enough in what you can do that you're not afraid to own up to the things that you can't, and to be able to keep your calm when people around you achieve perfection in an area of their lives without fear or envy or beating yourself up for being lesser. Editing your life to be authentic is a process that will help you become who you want to be, and to make the changes and do the work necessary in an efficient, thoughtful and realistic way. This might mean deconstructing the persona you've built, taking off your mask, speaking up for your happiest and healthiest self and being vulnerable – while setting boundaries. Once you start to get real and undergo an authentic edit of your life, you'll realise there is no such thing as perfection. We're all a little bit flawed, and those of us who know it can stop the competing, the crowing, or worrying about being usurped – we can get real and get on with life.

Authenticity:

- Not false or copied.
- Representing one's true nature and beliefs.
- Being true to oneself.
- Living in the moment and being present.
- Sharing your genuine thoughts and real feelings.

Edit:

- To prepare something (yourself!) for public presentation.
- To assemble by cutting and rearranging.
- To alter, adapt or refine specially to suit a particular purpose.
- To delete.
- To transform for the better.

A conversation with a friend who'd recently challenged herself to perform a life inventory reminded me that when our days are filled with the wrong and the *meh*, little room is left for self-restoration and self-preservation.

'Too many people around me found it too easy to be inconsiderate, inauthentic or greedy and not place any value on my time, needs or energy, and it made me question my own judgement about everything,' she said. 'Then, over the last couple of years, I felt a similar energy ricochet around the world, on a global scale, from leaders and politicians and movements, and on social media, and I got quite depressed.'

'How did you handle this realisation?' I asked her.

'I've found that I can often do without people. I've retuned myself. And I've stopped watching the news. Some people don't approve, but I've realised that I don't care.'

My friend stopped wasting her time on those who didn't treasure her, on systems and groups built on lies, and she switched off her television and social media, and started feeling safer. She got herself a new life motto, too: *Be nice to your truest self. It's hard to be happy when someone's being unkind to you all the time. Especially if that person is you.* She finally accepted herself, and started to treasure her story and accomplishments, which helped her to take care of her mental and physical health.

Enough is enough

Adulting is hard. And you know what else is hard? Recognising that moment when you've done enough and built enough – and that *you are enough.* Slow down enough to take a genuine look behind you with pride, take a few deep breaths and plan your route. Many people I meet have catapulted themselves towards unhealthy pursuits since they can remember: they strive to be richer, thinner and more popular with the in-crowd. They drive themselves wild for a bigger house, a bigger car, a better wardrobe. They think that there will be some final box to tick that says 'you're approved', and if they have children, they then propel these pressures of perfection onto their offspring. But too often, these people – and I was one of them in my teens, twenties and early thirties – get to the self-erected finish line and they don't feel happy, healthy, fulfilled and content. They look for what is next. They start looking for another finish line, or they're eyeing up their fellow competitors and doubting their own accomplishments; or they wonder if it was all worth the effort, pain and loss that they felt along the way, and then they take the edge off the flat feeling inside with unhealthy habits or unhelpful social circles.

I know. I lived this story; I wrote myself a plot and gave myself some killer dialogue. I introduced scandalous characters and allowed myself to make silly decisions to give me subconscious cliffhangers. And then one day I woke up. I stopped and stared long and hard at the manuscript of my life, then I picked up a pencil, made notes, did some research, scribbled out things that didn't make sense, or felt untrue, and I edited myself to a stronger place. No, this wasn't a one-time only reworking. I am *constantly* editing myself to a stronger, kinder, calmer, more accepting place. I realised that if my life was my masterpiece, it deserved my discerning eye, my gut instinct and my often painful but meaningful reflection. Each one of us owes ourselves that honour: to refuse to strive to be someone we are not.

My inauthentic life

When I performed my self-edit, those around me were shocked. No one could believe what I had done. What had I done that was so shocking? I'd turned down a million-dollar salary, left the very swanky corner office on Sixth Avenue in Manhattan I'd occupied for five years and packed up my hipster apartment in Brooklyn to move to a dilapidated ranch in Kentucky to try freelance writing and get an MA in English. Everyone (nearly everyone) thought I was having a mental breakdown. I'd conscientiously worked my way up the journalism ladder at various London glossies and newspapers since leaving university, and landing the title of editor-in-chief of *OK!* magazine in New York, aged 29, had felt like reaching the stars. I held a coveted position; I was envied, respected and I knew it. But I'll let you into a secret: deciding to turn my back on all that influence, material wealth and power wasn't because of a mental break*down*, it was because of a mental break*through*.

After half a decade feeling the heavy weight of pressure and responsibility, of tight deadlines, office politics, constant drama, and sleepless nights, I knew I'd had enough. A week wouldn't go by without someone threatening to sue me, or fire me, or leak a fabricated story about me or my team to a gossip website. The magazine market was going in a direction that made me feel a bit grim, more salacious and judgemental, a tone I hadn't signed up for and didn't feel authentic spearheading. But what I appeared to have was so seductive ... it was everything I'd ever worked for. I'd reached the pinnacle of the publishing world, selling one million magazines per week in the most competitive print market on the planet, and I was *friends* with the stars of Hollywood, giving Britney Spears elocution lessons and discussing the unmitigated pleasure of stepping into a London black cab with George Clooney. Anything I wanted at my fingertips. When my baby brother turned 21, I flew him into LAX to spend the day hanging out at the Playboy Mansion, then swung by the Staples Center to watch the LA Lakers, before hosting a dinner for him courtesy of Wolfgang Puck at Beverly Hills' hottest restaurant with a table full of witty, wonderful actors. I knew I was being given access to a crazy beautiful world way beyond my nerdy, working-class childhood dreams ... and yet I was miserable, grey, morally confused and flat. I remember at the time likening my life to that of Henry VIII, which probably sounds ridiculous, but I saw myself as being in the centre of this court, fawned over and pampered by court jesters and sycophants, over-indulged and praised, relying on a few key advisers to whisper wise words into my ear, but never really knowing what affection and respect was real and what was because of my title and influence. I found myself being quite untrusting and anxious. No heads rolled due to these unnerving emotions, but I was bloated with boredom (bizarrely, perhaps, I found it very difficult to get excited by celebrity shenanigans), doubt and insecurities.

My background was very unregal. Although society programmes us to desire money, power, praise and promotion, my childhood had imprinted a different focus on me. Growing up during the 1980s in the East End of London I queued up for lumpy mashed potato and even lumpier semolina in the free school lunch line alongside the other unfortunates – the kids with single mums like me or the kids who had just arrived in the country with nothing. I was aware that I was supposed to feel shame because we weren't welloff – the glossy girls with their pristine Club Sport tracksuits and stuffed My Little Pony lunch boxes had already learnt to sneer at the likes of me – and I did feel it, but I also saw what excess did to people and how kindness didn't come with a price tag. These girls who bullied me because I didn't have the coolest clothes or the latest toys, or a dad at home, didn't seem happy. Happy people weren't mean to others. These girls had everything handed to them on a plate, while my mum had to work for everything she could give us, yet I'd never heard her be mean about anyone, and she glowed from the inside out with a calm beauty that the other mothers, who bounced straight from fancy gyms to the school gates in the latest Air Jordan's, didn't possess. I now know what it was: it was the glow of authentically accepting her life as it was, its troubles and its comforts.

My mother's idea of success was having enough money left over after bills to buy fresh fruit at the end of each week and to take us on a two-week holiday every summer, which seemed like sensible goals to me. We didn't have much, but we were content. Believe me, I had other issues because of our social standing, which I'll share in the next chapter, but a reliance on material wealth and consumer goods was not in my wheelhouse. My mother's – and therefore my – happiness, I appreciated by the age of ten, came from small treats, kindness and companion-ship, married to purpose and peace. My mother never envied the mock-Tudor mansions that came with turbulent relationships acquired by her girlfriends; she had pulled up the eggshell carpet we'd been walking on from our modest home straight after my dad moved out, and replaced it with smooth, straight floorboards we could trust not to trip up on.

Straight after rejecting my boss's one million dollar offer to stay at the magazine, I walked out into Times Square to take a few deep breaths and call my mum. 'Well done,' she exclaimed without missing a beat as I told her about the money. 'Buying more designer suits and eating in fancy restaurants won't make you happy, nor surrounding yourself with these disingenuous flatterers. You need to look after your health and well-being in a real way.' No one else's reaction was as mindful and positive. The general consensus was that I must be mad to give up the title, the cash, the sycophants, the attention.

I wasn't mad. I was 34 and awash with ennui and living on my nerves. I didn't know the phrase 'adrenal fatigue' then, but that's probably what was happening. I knew my proper relationships needed nurturing, not the inauthentic ones built on a projected image of my perfect life and job title with A-listers and hangers-on. My self-worth was built on Christian Louboutin heels, not inner confidence, and that had to change. We were heading towards the peak of the Kardashian era – indeed Kim was my beauty editor-at-large – and as my world got more flashy, fake and full of itself, I felt queasy. I made a list of the things that I valued, how much money I needed to survive, and what I could cut back on. A lot, it turned out. My life was full of fluff, stuff and nonsense that didn't boost me, just my bank balance and my wardrobe. I researched the idea of happiness, looking for advice from people I admired. I'd met Richard Branson a few months earlier at a party, and I knew him to be a person who had found balance. 'Too many people measure how successful they are by how much money they make or the people they associate with,' he wrote. 'In my opinion, true success should be measured by how happy you are.' I knew he was right.

I walked away from my life of freebies and fabulosity, and moved to the American South to sway on a porch swing and watch fireflies dance at sunset with my husband. I went from sitting in the front row at New York Fashion Week chatting to the cast of *Sex and the City*, to sitting in a launderette sharing saltwater taffy with toothless cowboys who gave me lessons on how to spot a liar and make sweet iced tea, and mostly, the FOMO, imposter syndrome and insecurities I'd battled against since childhood gave up their fight. In the nine years since I quit my 'dream job' I feel Western social values have started to catch up with my mindset. My decision to quit a life and job others dream of, which once was seen as mad, bad and rash, now seems brave and sensible. I've spent those years getting a PhD, raising two children, travelling, encountering people from all over the world who make my heart full and my head expand, and writing wellness books. None of this has made me rich, but it has given me real purpose and genuine contentment.

Revamp, revise, redraft

Of course, social media makes it hard to ignore where I *should* be. The peers I've grown up alongside in London and New York flash their successes in front of my face and I imagine the experiences I'd be having if I hadn't made the decision to jump from the expected ladder. I think of the money I didn't make and the stories I'd never get to tell. Admittedly, it sometimes feels disappointing to watch the Oscars in flannel pyjamas from my sofa when I attended them in glittering gowns for five years. I have to check in with myself regularly to stay alert to the things I truly value, and I've trained my eyes to see through the carefully curated lives of show-offs who, when I meet them in person, confess their fears about keeping up, staying slim, being relevant. In my life now, no one cares about my waist-to-hip ratio or my relevance, and I feel great relief that I am no longer driven by shallow, meaningless goals.

Looking back, I acknowledge that leaving my dream job was my big career life edit, my big fuck-you to the idea of pretending to be perfect and worthy of praise – but I've been consistently grappling with issues of self-worth since I was a child, sometimes allowing the real me to win. When I was nine, I stopped getting upset that I didn't possess the natural skill to be a gymnast and turned my spare time to writing – which I did have a flair for – instead. As a teen, I accepted that beautiful boy Daniel was never going to fall in love with me, so I found solace in his equally cute friend Ben, who I knew really, really liked me, and with whom I had more meaningful conversations anyway. At university, I sat for an honest chat with my tutor who advised me that – to my disappointment – mathematics was not my strong point, and if I switched my focus from my beloved economics to politics, I could probably earn a higher degree. I did, and I did. My professor taught me an important lesson: I wasn't settling, I was mindfully playing to my strengths.

As an adult, accepting and working around my imperfections – and not getting thrown off course by seemingly perfect people I encounter – has become an even more powerful method of coping with what life has given me. As soon as I realised that I did have control and power over my own destiny, I felt happier and healthier. I learnt in my twenties that I was only in competition with myself, no one else. I faced up to my fears – and gossip and criticism – and threw off my role as the perfect wife, escaping an unhappy marriage and making the difficult decision to divorce a man who was good but I was desperately ill-suited to. I edited out bad friendships, forgiving myself for not being able to make everyone like me. I edited out places – moving across the world and living in many different cities, holding up my hand when I got decisions wrong, until I found the right place to raise a family and build a home.

Turning down one million dollars and letting go of an impressive title and all that adoration was the life edit that really turns people's heads, though. Friends and ex-colleagues often ask how

I did it. How I dared accept my limits and weaknesses and save my mental health? How can they get off the hamster wheel of consumption, public approval and promotions? I always say this: sit with yourself, at your most bare and honest. Make a list of what you need and what you don't – people, places, material goods, traits, hobbies. Who do you truly like? What do you truly like to do? In black and white, your true goals will appear. Shut off from others' expectations of you and write down what you need to create a happy, healthy life and what you need to edit out to be able to sit comfortably with yourself as you are. It could mean eliminating people who make you feel lesser, a job that makes you restless with panic, a trait you're trying to possess that makes you feel like a phoney. Consult your diary: there is no rush to make changes – you have time. And do the maths: what changes can you afford to make, how can you budget happiness? And if a big salary is important to you, that's cool. If beautiful handbags and fast cars make you happy, work hard to get them. You *do* you. You *be* you. I've discovered the true secret to success is having the courage to become the person you believe you were meant to be – not the person you've been told you should become – and gently, judiciously editing your life to make sure you're not allowing other people's ideas of perfection to force you into dark corners. And honestly, there is no time like the present.

You're all good

This book will be a blueprint to bravery, self-acceptance and moving on and moving up; a guide to stepping away from your own restraints and others' expectations to create the life you deserve; a calming mix of ideas and solutions that are easy to follow and feel genuine; anecdotes that are inspirational and direct. Each chapter will teach you how to balance your mental and physical health, manage a career with family and friends, and let go of the things that no longer serve you or the people you love. As you read, I want you to imagine all the bad things that have happened to you, picture them mushed up in your inner magic pot, until they are boiled down into an appreciation for what you *really* want and need to be happy and healthy.

Over the pages of this book, I will repeatedly ask you to accept your imperfections and the aspects of your life that need to be changed, and give you the skills, tools and confidence to say so, backed up with real-life evidence from people who have learnt to do just that.

You will learn to:

- Unlock your life's true purpose.
- Upgrade your ability to learn from mistakes, upsets or failures.
- Reduce limiting beliefs that have kept you trapped in unhealthy cycles.
- Develop new skills, strengths and habits.
- Define your life goals, priorities and core values.
- Improve your thinking to expand your self-awareness.
- Find a balance that works for you without harming others.
- Find your truth (not accept anyone else's).

As I share my journey to a happier life, and you read anecdotal advice from other people who are working towards self-kindness and self-love, I will coach you towards finding your voice and your ability to say yes to things that you want, no to things you don't, and cutting back on the unwanted to leave space for you to live happily and healthily in your own skin.

In each chapter, there will be opportunities for you to journal and note your thoughts, ideas and the changes you wish to make. I will:

- Ask open- and closed-ended questions so that you can clearly assess your needs, wants and desires. I encourage you to write down your answers. You will forget them, and it will be useful to return to them at intervals to see how you have edited your life to accept your limits and embrace your strengths – or not!
- Encourage you to think around each chapter's theme, bringing up real-life examples of inconsistencies, niggles or flare-up points in your life.
- Aim to raise your self-confidence and self-belief. When you feel good about yourself and your abilities, you'll feel more able to make positive, proactive decisions.
- Provide you with alternative solutions, perspectives and insights with which to compare your current life and your imagined life.
- Offer ideas to help you overcome potential roadblocks that you feel sit between you and your calmer, more contented routine.
- Challenge the limitations you have placed on your mental and physical health.
- Check your authenticity when thinking about your weaknesses. Are you listening to your gut?

As you go from page to page, I hope you can face your strengths and weaknesses with authenticity and honesty. This requires a lack of vanity, defensiveness or pretentiousness. This requires open-mindedness, realism and a proactive approach to being an agent in your own growth. At the end of each chapter, there'll be an authenticity checklist to help you think about your actions and how they're affecting your life, encouraging you to note down your aims, goals and ideas, and helping you to focus on what you need to add or eliminate to own your story and create your masterpiece: a life you love. As you read the anecdotes from people who have performed a successful life edit – creating more space for people and pursuits they truly value and nurture their finest qualities – you should reflect upon the lessons they've learnt that you could introduce into your own life.

Trigger warning

Major work on the self needs a strong stomach, whoever we are, however much we know it is needed. Dipping and delving into our memories and feelings can be brutal, and we never know what is going to bring us to our knees. Over the 12 months I've been researching this book, questioning every decision I've made, analysing it for its authenticity, while reading and listening to people I respect who are bravely displaying their truth to the world, triggers have seemingly popped up from nowhere, the tears springing from my eyes and down my cheeks so suddenly that I have not known what to do with myself, or how to heal myself quickly enough to carry on with my day. What the last year has taught me is this: a true reveal of self involves true grief – reliving hurtful comments to work out why they were so painful and what my reaction says about me at my core.

That's right: accepting what you can't do or don't do well is a tough core workout. It's going to make you uncomfortable, terribly sad at times, regretful over friends not cherished or words not spoken, and you'll realise how any deep self-reflection, followed by self-acceptance and new hope, is a journey. Because even when you are on your knees, or sobbing on the bathroom floor in the dark because you are misunderstood, lonely or in pain, or humiliated because you've turned a perfectly nice lunch with friends into a clashing confrontation of opinions because you're carrying so much emotional weight, you are growing. You are getting closer to good health and happiness, and further away from caring about things that don't matter. Be gentle with yourself; be kind.

Ultimately, *Get Real* requires you to be optimistic. My hope is that, over the course of this book, you give yourself permission to say no, say yes, cut back, fight back, listen up, look up, remove guilt and add joy. Focus on *your* idea of right and wrong, *your* idea of good and bad, *your* idea of what's cool and what's for fools, and the person you want to be – because you have to live with *you*, first and foremost. And you have a responsibility to yourself in all its messy, discombobulated, glorious truth.

Own your truth

As I was finishing writing this introduction, I got a text message from a friend. She'd had on-and-off battles with alcohol for the last decade, and finally, after over a year of being sober, she was sharing her troubles with friends, in person and on social media. The previous day I'd told her how I admired her honesty, that her open and often painful discussions and observations were probably helping more people than she could ever imagine. She told me that she'd had some feedback, some positive, some negative, but that she was OK with that.

'My grandma used to say to me "What other people think of you is none of your business",' she wrote, 'so if people feel uncomfortable with my truth, so be it. I don't focus on it. Their issues with *me* are nothing to do with *me*. I'm sharing my imperfections to keep me on track, and for the lonely one per cent who are invisibly struggling with drinking. If I had an emotional reaction to everything said about me or thought about me, I'd be a wreck, but I can't control anyone else, so I've let it go – and I've found a community that I can have a positive impact on.'

That's just one of the many ways living an authentic life can make you happier and healthier: your authenticity will help and inspire people who genuinely need you. And why be perfect when you can be helpful, happy and healthy? It turns out that life really is too short for fake friends, fake smiles, fake anything … and getting to your place of truth is really good for the soul!

Chapter 1

Once Upon a Time ...

'No matter who you are, no matter what you did,
no matter where you've come from, you can always change,
become a better version of yourself.'

Madonna

Do you have a plan that is working for you, or do you keep
making the same mistakes? If it's the latter, you're not alone.
We seem to be programmed to fuck up, again and again, don't
we? We make the same bad choices, with replica people, with
similarly disappointing results. Often, as adults, we live in sim-
ulacrums of our unhappy childhoods, aware that it didn't work
back then for us but unable to stop ourselves from recreating
them for our own offspring. Einstein is credited with stating
'the definition of insanity is doing the same thing over and
over again and expecting a different result' to which I say: life
has got so insane that we're just trying to keep up and survive –
can you blame us? Our souls are crying out for ease and peace,
but we're finding it hard to stay still long enough to listen to

them. There are too many external demands (work, education, social life, parenting), and there's too much external pressure (to be ambitious, skinny, popular, beautiful). Sadly, this is often put on ourselves *by* ourselves. We have inner demons telling us that we're not good enough, not smart enough or not attractive enough, so we hide our more authentic self under layers of disguise – mentally, socially, physically. We then distract ourselves from our true calling with bad habits or by burying ourselves in our work, or obsessing over other people's lives, all while repeating the same, unworkable routines because we're too scared to try something new. Sticking our head in the sand works for a while. We're distracted by a bit of gossip and glamour, or drama and intrigue, or by a series on Netflix and a bottle of Sancerre, and we forget to think too deeply about anything. But at some point, when your health is suffering or you're feeling alone despite having 1,000 Facebook friends, it will catch up with you. Living inauthentically can lead to suffocation.

Why a life edit is a good idea

If you're feeling stressed, anxious, unhappy, burnt-out or even just a little lacklustre, you could probably do with a life edit. Unhelpful roadblocks to a happier life build up over time without us realising sometimes, and they need to be acknowledged, analysed and removed. When you begin to edit out the mistakes, bad habits, cruel characters and negative influences, you'll be amazed by how much lighter you'll feel. It's hard at first. But there's good news. Recent research uncovered by a team at

University College London shows that it takes on average 66 days to form a habit, for a process to go from unnatural to automatic. This means that if you heartily start to edit new thoughts and actions into your daily routine, within three months you will have created a life you love, or at least, love a bit more: a life that won't lead to burnout, or anxiety, or a general feeling of *blah*. This first chapter will focus on why editing your life is a necessary requirement of building and maintaining the life you deserve, with tips on how to create the right diving board to launch yourself from.

I have always been editing my life, so it's no wonder that I chose to become an editor in my professional life. At first, I edited through fear. I would edit someone out of my life quickly – first – before they could cut me out, because my feelings of unworthiness and non-belonging led me to think that they always would. Or I would edit my authentic self to be lesser, more hidden, in case I drew attention to myself. I knew why I did it. It's because I had serious father issues, which had left such huge holes in my heart and confidence, I could not reveal my legit self for fear of being deemed unlovable. If I showed the real me, people would leave, I assumed, so I lied, denied, stayed silent and generally rebuked authenticity just to survive. But living a lie is exhausting, and not good for your mental health. A psychological study of 110 adults by a team at the University of Notre Dame uncovered that even white lies produced physical symptoms such as headaches, sore throats, muscle tension and stress, while encouraging people to be truthful at all times relieved the participants' mental and physical complaints. Lying, the study corroborated, triggers the release of stress hormones and increases heart rate and blood pressure. It takes a lot of negative energy to live an inauthentic life – as I knew all too well.

Question your motives

A quick check-in that you can do in any place, at any time, when a decision needs to be made, is to check your motives and only appeal to your best, most honest self. Why am I trying to make friends with this person? Why do I want to go there? Why am I treating someone I love that way? Normally – dissected – insincere motives fall into one of three categories: fear, envy or anger. These are not healthy reasons, so when choosing between yes and no, and you only have a few seconds, think motives, motives, motives.

Filling a father-shaped hole – and finding my authentic self

My greatest professional life edit was when I left my grand job as a magazine editor in New York City. My greatest personal life edits occurred the moment I became a parent, when I looked into my newborn son William's eyes for the first time and I knew that I would die for him. The rush of unshakeable love was instant and from the first moment he arrived in my life, I couldn't imagine living without him. A glance at my husband told me that he felt the same. I remember wishing, in that pure, perfect moment, that my own father had felt the same way about me. Instead, he abandoned my mother for another woman when my baby brother was a few weeks old and I was merely six, a decision that had a detrimental effect on my ability to show the real me for decades.

Single-parent families weren't common in the early 1980s and I was aware that Dad not living at home made me different, somehow less fortunate and freakish, queuing in the separate line for children who got free meals at lunchtime and noticing pitying glances at the school gates as I walked home alone because my mum, who was working three jobs, sometimes couldn't be there. I was jealous of my friends and their doting fathers, holding their hands, swinging them around in the air and telling them that they were beautiful. I put on a brave face and started telling myself my first lie: I didn't care. After he left home, I would spend every Saturday waiting by the front door with great anticipation for my father to show up for his court-appointed visit. He went through a phase of buying me a Care Bear as an apology every time he didn't show up. Soon I had the whole Care Bear collection. I remember one weekend I was particularly excited because he had promised to take me to a Spurs game at White Hart Lane. He gave my ticket to his current flame and my mother tried to console me with a video – *Annie*. It's a film that I still hate with a passion.

On the few times when he did turn up, the promised day trips never materialised. Instead, I'd be taken to the homes of various new girlfriends and plonked in front of a television while my father disappeared into a bedroom. I remember the crushing weight of being irrelevant to him, even now. Men are supposed to adore their daughters but he showed no interest in me. His reaction directly affected my personality at this crucial time: I would blush constantly, convinced that anything I had to say must be worthless or wrong. I became shy, because if your own father ignores you, why would anyone else pay you attention? And – most damagingly in the long term, I believe – I lost faith in my ability to be loved. His action made me view my authentic self as worthless, and so I covered myself up in lies, silenced my voice. No one was I lying more to than myself.

Childhood and the authentic self: an expert's view

'Fathers play a critical role for girls growing up, establishing a woman's strong sense of self. When they provide positive life principles, their daughters are better equipped to face life's challenges and believe in their own credibility,' explained Jennifer Blair, a life coach and author of *The True You: Tools to Excavate, Explore and Evolve*, who I visited shortly after my son's birth when all these feelings sprung up again, raw and tangible, after years of being buried and ignored. As the fellow child of divorce, she understood all too well how pre-teen daddy issues can resurface in adulthood. 'Dads usually push harder, and when a father encourages and inspires his daughter, he helps to create a sense of accomplishment which contributes to a solid self-confidence. Young girls also receive their sense of safety and security from their fathers. When fathers do what they say they are going to do, trust is established. Living with integrity means "action meeting words" and this is one of the quickest ways to be validated and assured that you are worth something from a toddler onwards. During my decade coaching, I have observed a common theme among female clients who have struggled much of their lives with unhealthy self-esteem due to a missing or disinterested father,' Jennifer told me. 'They lack assurance and believe that they don't do enough, don't have enough, and are not enough – so they run their lives in a way that is exhausting and unfulfilling. These silent daughters can appear to be successful in many ways, but often do not feel like their inside and outside matches. They are constantly trying to fill the hole left in their lives by their father's absence from their childhood. They desperately seek love, attention, and acceptance from others, rather than being authentic.' This was me to a tee.

Smells like teen dispirit

Around my tenth birthday, four years after her divorce, my mother started dating a man called Keith, their dates becoming more frequent as my natural father's interest in me hit an all-time low – I would go without seeing him for six weeks at a time. They were married within a year. I remember sitting in the front row of a London register office, with a beautiful bouquet and wearing a vintage velvet frock coat, thinking, 'I'll have to look after myself now. Mum will be busy looking after her new husband.' I assumed that I would be pushed to one side again. After all, if my real father didn't want me, why would a new one? A year later, I had a new baby brother. Now that he had a natural child who would automatically receive anything should my mother or he die, Keith – the decent, honest man he is – decided to look into legally adopting me and my other brother. Deep down, I assumed the thought of having his children adopted would kick my real father into reality. He'd rebel and fight to keep us and the promised trips to the football would begin. But I unfortunately overheard the social worker telling my mother that once he'd established that signing his rights away would mean he wouldn't have any financial responsibilities for us, he practically begged her for the pen. I cannot begin to reveal the damage this did me, at 13 years old – already struggling to forge an identity for myself in those tricky teenage years – and how much it delayed my ability to be real with myself and others.

A pattern quickly formed in my early relationships with the opposite sex: my deep-rooted paranoia that I was unlovable led me to end relationships because I was afraid that they would find the real me lacking in some way and dump me. When I fell in love for the first time aged 17, my insecurity spelt doom from the minute we got together. After worshipping Samuel from afar for over a year, within weeks of dating I stopped returning his calls and wouldn't show up where we'd agreed to meet. He, quite rightly, thought I was a lunatic. I was too scared to explain my fears – I wouldn't have known how to articulate them even if I was brave enough back then – and forced our fledgling coupling on to a path of destruction until it gradually hit a dead end. I cried for weeks, turning my lavender pillows deep blue with tears, only finding solace in my control over its death – and that I hadn't allowed it to go on too long. The ending would assuredly come, so at least I was getting on with the rejection on my own terms rather than having it thrust upon me. At university and throughout my twenties, my paranoia led to a different style of inauthenticity: I'd overcompensate. In a bid to cling on to the affections of a man – however unworthy – I'd concede to their whims, keep my mouth shut and put up with behaviour that a woman with a little more self-respect would call an end to, like drug taking, going missing for days on end and putting their friends first.

The joy and realisation of being a parent

It was honestly only when I became a parent myself that I fully understood that I didn't do anything to make my birth father leave and I didn't have to self-destruct every chance at happiness I was given. It was not my fault that he didn't love me or want to be a part of my life. I was just an innocent child who deserved the never-ending, unconditional love that most parents can offer from the first moment they look into their baby's eyes; the unconditional love I had felt when looking at my son for the first time. Finally, now, these roadblocks are removed, I edit through choice not fear: what best serves me and my family, our health and happiness? What should I cut out to make more time for things that benefit us? Alongside this familial resolution, there is a liberation to ageing that brings with it a natural culling, a confidence in your own skin. I found, as have most of my friends of a certain age, that as the number of candles on a birthday cake increases, the number of fucks given about other people's opinions decreases. These huge edits – and the minor ones I perform every day, week, year to keep my life going in the right direction – have been invaluable as I strive to be the best mother, partner, friend and collaborator that I can be.

Words to the wise

Here are ten books that capture a character's inner integrity at the moments they make great changes and difficult choices:

- *My Brilliant Friend* by Elena Ferrante
- *Circe* by Madeline Miller
- *Becoming* by Michelle Obama
- *I am, I am, I am* by Maggie O'Farrell
- *Motherwell* by Deborah Orr
- *Like Water for Chocolate* by Laura Esquivel
- *The Liar* by Stephen Fry
- *Me* by Elton John
- *Austerlitz* by W. G. Sebald
- *Born a Crime* by Trevor Noah

Are you blocking your best self?

We all have baggage. As you have just read, I have enough suitcases of pain, insecurity and self-doubt to fill a carousel at Heathrow Airport. The best we can do is acknowledge it and send it packing.

How can you build your self-confidence? It can start with the smallest of daily edits. Let's start with the seemingly trite, which work as quick boosts. Make sure that you dress in a way that makes you feel comfortable and smart; not expensively necessarily, just good about yourself. Daily grooming rituals can help with this, too – feel fresh with a shower, clean skin, a spray of invigorating oils, wearing a smile when possible. Remember that good posture helps you to (figuratively and literally) stand tall. Invest in a good haircut and skincare, and shoes that put a spring into your step. From the external to the internal, think positive, be positive, give positively. Being kind and generous to others makes you feel better about yourself. Look for solutions rather than problems. And never stop finding ways to improve: studies prove exercise, a love of learning and gratitude all push you to believe that you are worth self-investment. We'll get on to the value of who you call friends and how they can boost your self-confidence in Chapter 6.

You little tinker!

Your life is your masterpiece, your greatest work, your story in action, so don't be ashamed or scared to tinker around with it, play with your options and admit that you've come to a deadend and need to redirect yourself. Tinkering keeps you on your toes. It makes you adaptable, reflective, brave and experimental – these are all good qualities to have in every area of your life. Do a Darwin: believe in evolution!

Small changes are still *powerful* changes. Fiddle around with what suits you, until you find the right balance. Life edits don't have to be daunting. Many people benefit from tiny tweaks such as keeping a gratitude journal, or walking up the stairs instead of taking the lift, or setting their alarm clock half an hour earlier each day to stretch and drink coffee in silence before the madness of the day begins. Others find peace of mind in completing minuscule tasks regularly and efficiently: washing dishes immediately rather than letting them build up in a dirty heap, replying to an email when received instead of putting it off and then worrying about forgetting it, sorting out lunches and water bottles for the following day in the evening rather than in a panicked morning rush, making their bed the minute they haul their body out of it. These are all insignificant edits that can build to make your life calmer. Bold edits like stopping smoking or leaving an unhappy marriage are wonderful, of course, but don't set yourself such monumental tasks that you are scared to get started. Every tiny step is taking you in the right direction.

Writing the book of you

Every professional writer can tell you that the first piece of advice they are given by their peers when looking down the barrel of a blank page, is to 'write about what you know'. The general assumption when this remark is offered is that the thing you know most about is yourself, so that is where any great story should start. As a bookish nerd from the moment I could read, I have always viewed my life as a collection of short stories, rather than a novel. There are different experiences that set up and enhance themes and the recurring protagonist's (or my own!) temperament and disposition, without being cemented to a particular narrative. How about taking a look at your life right now like this, too? What would you want readers to think about the book of you? Narrowing down your desires, cutting back on surplus characters and curtailing unhealthy plotlines are all must-dos if you want your life to become your personal version of a bestseller. At the beginning of the life-editing process, we can break down this process – your masterpiece – into three digestible chunks. Keep your answers close to hand as you work through each chapter:

1 Do your research

Take a good look at your current life – the pluses and the minuses. Note them down. Consult your diary and analyse what is taking up your time. Look through your contacts list: what immediate feeling springs into your heart when you see a family member or close friend's name? Joy, displeasure or indifference?

Take an inventory of things in your life story that you no longer need Are some people in the outer circle of your life troublemakers, naysayers, pessimists or irritants? Do they have any upsides, or are they energy vampires who you would be better off without as you create a life you love? Are you carrying the weight of your ancestors like I was? Dump it. Do some places make you nervous, uneasy or restless? Do you have to keep going there? Are there locations better suited to the life you wish to lead?

Take an inventory of things in your life story that you want to build upon and nurture Do you tell people who you love that you love them enough? How about showing your appreciation and affection more? Can you try building out time in your day/week/month/year for those who you adore? Do you spend enough time outside? It always makes you feel better – those fresh phytoncides (a substance emitted by trees to help them protect themselves, and that can help humans too), that vitamin D or cobweb-sweeping sea air – so how about boosting your intake? Do you get enough alone time? How would you feel if you read more, swam more, danced more, sang more? Good, right? Better! Some things, as you authentically edit your life, you need to *stop* saying yes to and some things you need to *start* saying yes to – you need to balance your physical and emotional scales.

2 Lay out your chapter plan

Where do you want your story to go? Do you have a conclusion in mind – the final reveal that ticks all your boxes? If so, note down your route. If not, list your firm must-nots instead. What things make you really unhappy and stressed, and how can you avoid them in the long term?

What bucket-list items do you want to include? Fast forward 30, 40 years into the future, to your deathbed. What things would you be gutted not to have achieved or seen? Time flies faster than you think. Plan ahead: what adventures or attributes do you want to weave into the book of you?

How can you manage your mental health as you go through these life edits? Know your limits. You are enough, so life editing isn't about adding more for the sake of it. Money and power really don't make you happy, so don't chase them to the detriment of your health. Treat yourself gently and kindly. That could be by carving out time in your busy life for a daily bath with a locked door; to hiring a life coach or going for a weekly therapy session. Self-care is not a wellness phase but a sensible decision.

Getting to a happy ending Allow yourself the time to day-dream, plot and muse upon what your happiest life would look like and how your last chapter could tie loose ends together.

3 Fill in the blank pages

Think carefully about the tone you wish to set across all aspects of your life. How would you like your friends to describe you? Do you value courage and fortitude over humility and conscientiousness?

How will you deal with the villains in your life story, while becoming your own hero? What principles do you wish to build into your life story? What characteristics make you feel proud of yourself?

How do you want your life story to be interpreted and enjoyed by others? Imagine you are an observer of your life, or a reader of the book of you. What do you think would stand out? How could some of your traits be misinterpreted, undervalued or ignored? How can you change your actions and behaviours to get the reaction you feel you merit?

How to set realistic expectations for your future

Compiling a life you love – filled with people who deserve you – takes time, effort and patience. Your fears, worries and insecurities can flare up at any point, triggered by the face of a person who reminds you of a school bully, or an interaction with a stranger that unleashes past annoyances. Be aware of your limits, without being intimidated by them. Don't over-promise yourself to people when you need time to address your own aims and goals. 'Under-promise and over-deliver' is something my grandma used to say to me. She was talking about her work as the accessories manager at a busy London department store, but I took it on board as something far more personal: don't boast, show off, guarantee. Just work hard and get the job done calmly and quietly. It's better to surprise others – and yourself – in a positive way, than in a negative way.

Before you take on a challenge, familiarise yourself with potential obstacles. Do you have the time, energy, resources, willpower or ability? If you're missing one vital link, how can you compensate? Set yourself a timeline for change, but don't get the date engraved in stone. Be flexible, within reason. Have a plan, but don't throw the baby out with the bathwater if you get off to a slow start or hit a few road bumps along the way. Finally, check in with yourself. Your goals could change. You might, halfway through a life edit, find something more rewarding or meaningful to focus on, or an unexpected issue or problem could halt your progress. Never stop asking yourself if you're OK, and if you want to carry on.

Journal your journey – your goals

Stop here for a minute and pick up a pen. Right now, note down in a notebook your healthiest goals. Think and write down what you want to focus on most in this moment. Add the date, note your mood, and reflect on what you've written here as you move on through the chapters.

Getting real: Lara, 35

'I've found that when I'm feeling really burnt out, particularly on the daily grind type of things (chauffeuring, supervising homework, making dinner that gets rejected), it usually means that I am not doing anything for myself and it's time to be a little bit "selfish". Yes, it's the yoga and hot baths, etc., of self-care, but it also usually means that I need to work on a project or set aside some time to do something that is fulfilling or meaningful or enjoyable to *me*. We make so many sacrifices and compromises as parents that sometimes it just really helps to do something that is not a sacrifice or a compromise. It can be as big as working on a creative personal project or as small as saying, "No, we're going to watch the movie *I* want to watch today." It makes me feel a bit more like an actual human being!'

Heart in art

Here are ten movies that capture authenticity with tender care and insight, with some valuable life lessons thrown in:

- *Call Me by Your Name*
- *12 Years a Slave*
- *Erin Brockovich*
- *Vera Drake*
- *The Florida Project*
- *The Imitation Game*
- *A Beautiful Mind*
- *Wonder*
- *Coco*
- *Up*

Nothing compares to you

When you imagine a life that you will love, are you thinking deeply and realistically about what you really do love? Or are you thinking about socially acceptable ideas about what others would need to create a life that they love? Keeping up with the Joneses is exhausting and often meaningless, because we never truly know what is going on behind the shiny, bright exterior. What might look perfect and dreamy to you – be it a marriage, a home, a job or a body – from the outside, could be a nightmare in reality. That is why when undergoing an authenticity edit you need to focus on what is real, pure and credible for you – no one else. Remember:

No one is perfect You are comparing yourself to a fantasy. Even your flashbacks aren't foolproof. You might look back on family holidays as wonderful and worry that you won't give your kids the same joyful memories each summer, but you've probably glossed over airport delays, food poisoning and constant squabbling. Treasure your memories, but don't be fooled or ruled by them.

Social Media is largely BS We are seeing a perfectly crafted snapshot of a moment, not the whole truth. The messy, inglorious, frazzled truth doesn't get so many likes. I find the faux truth is often the most depressing. 'Oh, you caught me with no make-up on and so stressed because I have three parties to go to tonight.' Purlease. (a) they have make-up on; and (b) three parties sounds like a lot of hassle. Don't fall for the fictional displays of the vain or needy, and if you must engage, know it for what it is: an image they want you to see.

We all have different advantages, and disadvantages, because life isn't fair. Comparing ourselves to others is fruitless because some people will always have more than us, which makes us resentful, and some will always have less, which makes us feel guilty. Circumstances fluctuate: we all have good and bad times. I have reset my mindset so that when a friend tells me news that I would once feel envious of, I rejoice in it, thankful that there are still opportunities out there, and I use it as motivation to achieve my goals. If I am envious, I tell them so – it's how I truly feel – but when it's out in the open, the light makes my jealousy laughable, rather than weird and sad as it would if I allowed it to fester away in the dark. Freeing yourself from a comparative mindset will allow you to focus on what you are doing, and how you are doing it. Doing this allows me to ask for advice or suggestions about self-improvement from people I trust and admire, rather than shirking away from their successes.

Comparing ourselves to others is all a waste of time anyway. Buddhism tells us that fundamentally all humans have to go through the same four phases of life, regardless of money, power or beauty. We are born, we age, we get ill and we die – all of us, no matter if we got that sought-after handbag before our friends, or we recorded a better training ratio than our colleagues. What matters, teaches the Buddha, and what makes our existence worthwhile, is self-acceptance, authentic relationships and a clear purpose. We can only get this from within. It doesn't matter what the woman next door has parked on her driveway or the woman on the desk next to you gets for Valentine's Day.

Beautiful and balanced

When it comes to starting off on an even keel, research shows we need fewer high-octane thrills and materialism excess, and more routine and gentle delight. These life edits have given me a simple joy in the day-to-day, which ricochets around my larger world like a billion rays of sunshine.

- Research published in the *World Leisure Journal* highlighted, when studying 751 British families, how the best predictor of familial joy came when quality leisure time was valued in the home, with members focusing on routines they could do together. Simple rituals increase security and contentment, and with that happiness. This research proves that you can cut back on the demands of an active social life, expensive holidays and luxurious gifts, and focus on quality time together.

- Being kind to others releases the feel-good hormone serotonin, so do a good deed. According to a study on happiness from the University of British Columbia, helping others can reduce social anxiety and boost joy, alertness and interest in life for up to four weeks. Being a good friend or volunteering helps you as much as anyone else.

- Silent contemplation has multiple benefits when living your best life. The *Journal of Science and Healing* reveals how meditation can alleviate an individual's stress and suffering, improving their psychological state and their quality of life. Quiet pastimes such as colouring, reading, watching movies or gardening, allow the brain to unwind and wander more than more frenetic leisure activities, giving you permission to cut back on the extra-curricular classes and sports sessions.

- Partake in meaningful conversations face to face rather than the shouting world of social media. The National Institute of Mental Health advise 'talk therapy' or counselling as a great way to start healing your way to happiness, and if that is not available, simply spending time and confiding in people who you trust to help you find solutions is invaluable.

- Boost your endorphins in a way that works for you.

A 2016 study by the University of Colorado showed a direct correlation between exercise and the psychological uplift in women's mood. Dance – it will reduce the stress hormone, cortisol, that's rushing around your body, while a leisurely hike in the woods or a walk on the beach only doubles the bliss, also giving you the connection with nature that is such a bliss-bringer, states *Frontiers in Psychology*.

- Never edit out good sleep hygiene. The *Journal of Sleep Research* studied women for two weeks and found a direct correlation between good-quality sleep and greater happiness, and decreased levels of depression and anxiety. We'll discuss good rest more in Chapter 3.

Songs for your soul

Below are ten songs to make you sing, dance and remember that honesty is the best policy when it comes to living your healthiest, happiest life:

- 'Truth Hurts' by Lizzo
- 'The Cover is Not the Book' by Emily Blunt and Lin-Manuel Miranda
- 'Policy of Truth' by Depeche Mode
- 'Honest' by The Chainsmokers
- 'Thinking Out Loud' by Ed Sheeran
- 'Fast Car' by Tracy Chapman

- 'Love, Truth and Honesty' by Bananarama
- 'Honesty' by Billy Joel
- 'I Won't Back Down' by Tom Petty and The Heartbreakers
- 'I Honestly Love You' by Olivia Newton-John

Getting real: Summer, 40

'I like it when people manage my expectations, when they openly and authentically let me know in advance what I can expect from them, so I try to do the same for others. I am not impressed by the busiest, most involved or most stressed-out people in the room. If anything, I think that they haven't figured it out yet. Do what you can, do it authentically and you will be surrounded by the loveliest people who can also do this. Forget perfection and competition. Just live within your real values, abilities and fancies. I've stopped chasing everything and everyone; now I let things come to me.'

Own your story – here's how

This is where you check in and note, score and plan an outline for your most authentic life going forward. In this chapter we've covered the basics. You should ▶

now have looked at your current life and seen what you can change and why those cuts and edits would be a good idea.

Analyse your happiness

Is anything so nice that you would want to do it twice? Then do it.

Upgrade your habits

Do you get enough sleep, water, alone time, exercise?

Treat yourself kindly

Have you got a self-care routine in place?

Have faith in your core values

What do you need to boost to create a life that you love?

Expand your horizons

How do you want your final chapter to look?

Narrow down negative influences

Stop being driven by the envy of others, and focus on yourself.

Take time to improve your skills

Practise finding balance in the everyday.

Improve your thinking

Don't be too hard on yourself if you make a mistake and need to re-edit.

Cut back on pursuits that clutter

Life is short; spend it with people who make you laugh, feel loved and lift you up.

Chapter 2

Be Your Own Sunshine

'You wouldn't worry so much about what others think of you
if you realised how seldom they do.'

Eleanor Roosevelt

At some point, we all realise that there truly is no other option –
it's obvious. You have to be you, because everyone else really is
already taken. That doesn't mean that you can't borrow, imitate,
glean and grow from the gifts and insights you witness around
you, and delete the bits from yourself that you recognise as unfa-
vourable in others, but you really do have to claim ownership
of your own soul, purpose, goals, foibles and naughty bits: your
unique X-factor. I did this by learning to laugh at myself. When
you're a bit different from the norm, or you break the mould, or
you choose to stand up for yourself and others, you have to learn
to laugh at yourself. For me, it was a case of making the joke
and owning it before someone could turn it into a criticism – a
dagger to wound me with. As a child, I was the one who the bul-
lies teased with mean names – geek, nerd, bookworm, giraffe

(I've always been freakishly tall and ended up at 1.82m/6ft) – or making jokes about my family circumstances, and instead of thinking on my feet and owning their labels, I shrank, blushed, cried and felt lesser, embarrassment stopping me from telling anyone about the abuse. Since my late twenties I've made a point of owning my differences and sharing my limitations before anyone else could. Laughing at your mishaps means taking power into your own hands. Instead of being the joke, you become the joker. To be comfortable in one's own skin is a superpower.

Owning my mistakes and quirks is something I learnt from a beloved friend, in a swift statement that turned an awkward mishap into the moment I fell in love with her for ever. She and I were at a fabulous rugby ball, with a few other girlfriends and an obscene amount of beautiful men. We were both single, so this was rather exciting. We looked elegant and we felt fabulous. As we surveyed the room, our eyes fell on a number of handsome bachelors who we wanted to get to know better. We lifted our hems (it was all very Disney Princess) and started to descend the grand, sweeping staircase to enter the throng ... and she skidded, tumbled and rode her way to the bottom of the stairs with her dress up round her waist, Spanx on show. We looked down, mortified, as everyone stared. She stood up tall, shook herself down and with a glint in her eye as we rushed to meet her, she said without missing a beat, 'Sorry, girls, but you know I like to be the centre of attention.' How brilliant and sexy, and clever, and funny is that? A dashing lad brought her a glass of champagne and we laughed our way onto the dance floor. She taught me a lot about editing out embarrassment, fear and anxiety, and just embracing who you are, what you've done, and what you want to project – even in knicker-flashing moments. She also taught me a lot about silencing my *schaden-freude* sniggers and cutting out my gloating grin when observing others' cringeworthy moments. Bite your tongue. People in glass houses – which we all move into at different times in our lives – shouldn't throw stones.

The projection section

How do you want your life to look? What do you need to edit out, highlight, cut back on and say no to? What makes the pure you? In the first fog of motherhood, when I loved my new identity as a parent but wondered what that meant for my old, established identity, I carefully considered all the things that had built me into the person I was up until that moment, then I carefully curated the things I could (should!) lose and the things I could (would!) build upon, using this new, potent chapter in my life as an important time for a self-edit. How do these things project your self-image in the way that you want? Think about each one:

- Your memories up until this point
- Your experiences – personal and professional
- Your explorations, travels and adventures
- Your qualifications and assets
- Your relationships with friends
- Your relationships with family
- Your purpose and goals
- Your values and virtues
- Your moments of true joy

It is important to look at the key things to cut, too. What has wriggled its way into your life that is unhelpful or unnecessary? Sometimes in the rush of work, kids, promotions and nights in the pub, we mislay our intuition – a dangerous thing to do. A friend who had been through a year-long period of self-reflection, cutting corners and trimming down the superfluous to a point where she felt finally strong after a long period of depression, posted this on her Instagram recently: 'My intuition is so powerful I not only know who I am, I know who you are too.' I questioned her about it. 'I'm finally appreciating that I am not their opinion of me,' she said. Who were *they*? 'My parents, my social circle, my colleagues. I've got to the point where I can make a decision without worrying about other people, because what might be credible and legit for them, is not credible and legit for me.' Could she give me an example? She cut the bimonthly visits to the opera with her mum – an evening she dreaded – in exchange for a dinner where they could actually talk. A grateful neighbour who loved all things soprano got the spare ticket, her mother forged a new friendship of mutual interest that made her less reliant on her daughter as a buddy – which sometimes overwhelmed them both – and their mother–daughter relationship deepened in a tangible, healthy way for both of them. One small authentic edit, and the results rippled out in ever-increasing circles.

Where to look for meaningful inspiration

Sometimes it's easy to recognise the issues in your life, to know what you want to change, and to make it happen. Other times, life gets in the way. You're tired, stressed, insecure – or even just too hormonal or depressed to have faith in your own strengths and ability. In times like these, it can be helpful to look for inspiration from people or places around you. I know that when I am at my most depleted or doubtful, an escape into the peace and calm of the woods can reset my energy and focus, or a conversation with a friend who offers sound advice and a fresh perspective can be inspiring and motivational.

Daniel Chadborn and Stephen Reysen, psychologists at Texas A&M University, are experts in inspiration and its value in boosting creativity, as it 'acts as a motivational concept, in which inspiration is evoked (generated) from a source and a person then finds some means to transmit an idea and is driven to produce some creative outcome as a result'. They describe inspiration as having both a passive and an active aspect: we see someone do something we would be proud to do, or living on a higher level than us, and that leads us to want to add value to our lives. They believe, through their research, that being inspired by others you admire can really help to light an inner fire. They also acknowledge that you don't need to look for inspiration from those at lofty, unattainable heights, just from those who are doing a bit more than you, yet are still similar to you and who are personifying your goals. This could be the friend who has started running once a week who invites you to join her, or the neighbour who has lost a bit of weight and has offered to share her diet plan, or the colleagues who have stopped wasting time moaning and gossiping in the office so that they can get their work done and leave on time every day – these actions encourage you to do the same. All these examples show how low-key interactions with people you admire can boost and inspire you to live a life that is better suited to your aims and needs.

When searching for inspiration . . .

Don't give up on yourself too easily We all have rough times, sad times, lazy times. A day spent on the couch in pyjamas watching bubblegum television is sometimes needed. You might not be up for inspiration today but give it another go when you've had enough sleep or the sun is shining.

Be careful not to get yourself into a position of feeling jealous or envious of someone who could be inspiring you. Just because they have a better job, politer children, or a smaller bottom it doesn't mean that you're stuck with what you've got. Reject any *schadenfreude* vibes or bitterness, and ask yourself why they annoy or niggle you, and what you can learn from them.

Imitation is the sincerest form of flattery Don't feel guilty for copying someone else's ideas – just give them the credit they deserve for doing it first, and thank them.

Switch off It's hard to be inspired when you're constantly consuming social media, your brain buzzing with noise and drama. Take a mental break and daydream, embrace silence and allow your mind to wander. Mull over your goals, ideas and purpose.

Ask questions When you speak to someone who you find inspirational, interview them about their thought process or daily routine. I don't mean interrogate them, but don't feel shy when asking for tips. Most people will be flattered.

Read – every day. And I don't mean just your Facebook page (although I often find inspiration there, I admit). Read fiction and non-fiction, the memoirs of people you admire, the arts and culture sections of newspapers. Tear out pages, make notes and follow up with your own research. Refresh your ideas on a daily basis.

Collaborate Teamwork can make your dream work. If you're mentally or physically stuck in a rut, share your pain with others and get some group therapy. When I was feeling a bit lacklustre and antisocial, I started a book club and a film club to ensure that I read at least one book a month and saw at last one new film. The conversations and interactions that have come from this – from the piece of art itself, and the friends I consume it with – stretch my mind. Bounce ideas around with people you respect. Connectedness brings forth happiness, support and creativity. Don't be one-sided about it, however – be there to inspire others, too.

Travel Nothing changes an outlook or widens a perspective like seeing new places and different faces. Whenever you head somewhere new, be open to talking to locals, going off the beaten track (always putting safely first) and trying new things.

Trust your gut

Second-guessing yourself to the point of inaction is a dangerous habit that too many of us are trapped into again and again. In my twenties, I spent many hours – no, days! – worrying about what others would think of my choices, from things as innocuous as what I was wearing to serious life-changing events such as where I lived, who I dated and who I married. Apparently, this was a hereditary issue. When my mother got ready to marry my birth father at the age of 25, she knew that something wasn't quite right. She heard warning bells. Every time he let her down, she felt worthless. When he flirted with other women, or didn't fulfil a promise, she heard those bells. A dagger in her gut twisted. Her mother – my grandmother – asked her about those bells. Did she know what they meant? Deep down she did, but she didn't want to listen to her body. What she wanted was a charming, handsome husband and a 'normal' life: a home, a family, security. Despite her inner wisdom and her mother's concern, she married him, and a few years into the marriage, when his spitefulness brought her daily horror, the ringing in her ears was too loud to ignore. Although by this time she had a tiny baby (my brother) and a six-year-old (me) to support, she embraced her inner gut, told him to leave, and our little family was better off for her brave, authentic decision.

Oh, how history loves to repeat itself! I fell in love with my first husband at the same age my mother fell in love with my birth father. I was instantly impressed by his quick wit, fine brain and love for Broadway musicals. He wasn't my usual type, but my spirit had just been broken by the epitome of my usual type (a tall, fair, sporty lad with bucket-loads of swagger), so I stumbled, dragging my cracked heart and historically shattered confidence behind me, into his eager arms. And then, when 15 months later a ring was produced on a holiday in Rome, I loved the romance of it all – and the security, the comfort I felt that a man wanted me and wasn't going to leave. But flashing my diamond in my glossy magazine office the following Monday, an older – and I assumed at the time, bitter – female colleague, a confirmed singleton, made herself heard forcefully above the din of 'oohs' and 'aahs'.

'I might like Mars bars right now,' she philosophised within earshot. 'But in ten years' time I might fancy a Twix. Why would someone restrict themselves to a lifetime of routine sweetness in such a manner, at such a young age, when one hasn't really got to grips with who they actually are yet?'

I was furious at such condemnation, because deep down, something niggled that she was correct.

If I could go back, I'd tell my younger self to trust my gut and sample the whole sweet shop, then live without chocolate for a while, and then make a choice. My younger self wouldn't have listened though. Because at the time I hadn't honed my ability to trust my gut – or my parents, who were the only people as invested in my welfare as I was.

'We don't understand why you want to get married,' my mum pleaded with me at an emergency family conference when we'd just announced our engagement. 'You have everything to live for – both of you do – so why do you want to trap yourselves so early on into a relationship that could run its course in a few years.'

'How dare you! I love him!' I barked back.

'But, darling, listen to the warning bells in your head. Can you really not hear them? Do you really think this young man can make you happy for ever? Does he love you with all his heart?'

'I love him!' I repeated, dripping hot tears on to the vinyl tablecloth in the little café where the three of us were seated for this painful tête-à-tête. My caring stepfather, who I had called dad since I was 13, had chosen a public place on mutual territory in the hope of avoiding such dramatics.

'Well, you do now,' he questioned me gently.

'Always!' I bellowed. 'What do you know anyway?'

'Sadly, too much,' he replied. He too had lived through an unhappy marriage and a difficult divorce.

'I knew the marriage to your father was wrong, too,' my mother agreed, reaching over to take my stepfather's hand and giving it a squeeze. I knew they both found it hard to talk about their previous marriages in front of each other. 'I heard all these bells in my head, these warning sirens going off, yet I just pushed them away.'

'Well, I know what I'm doing,' I answered quietly, blowing my nose into a paper napkin. 'You can't judge me by your own mistakes. I'm going to the loo.'

As I flounced off I heard my dad say, 'He hasn't got enough life for Sarah though,' with a sadness in his voice that made me lock myself in that café's toilet for a considerable amount of time and weep over what I was about to do, knowing deep down that something wasn't right, and angry in that moment that he probably knew me better than I knew myself.

It is mistakes – big, like my romantic ones, and small, like wearing a terribly clingy pale blue dress that exaggerated my cellulite to an important event which would be photographed excessively for public distribution – that have taught me to listen to my head *and* my heart. And it works, as Oprah Winfrey attests: 'I've trusted the still, small voice of intuition my entire life. And the only time I've made mistakes is when I didn't listen.' Time has taught me to trust my gut, listen to warning bells, stop overthinking what other people want, or need, or approve of. Give yourself permission to know your truth.

Three steps to stop the indecision

1 **Ask yourself questions** Why are you feeling unsure? Why are you second-guessing yourself? Write it down. Make a list. Judge your assumptions and your prejudices. Evaluate the rewards versus the risks. Imagine your best, wisest self looking down on you and the choice you are making – taking in your history and your hopes for the future. This wider view can help you to pinpoint the challenge that is arresting your development. Argue with yourself! Be a devil's advocate – are you too defensive, too scared, too shy to do what should be done? Imagine that you are giving advice to someone you love. When making a big decision, all these processes will help you to align with your gut and help you to fine-tune your intuition to allow you to make decisions quicker – and better – in the future.

2 **Use everything you've got** Point one deals with logical questioning, now you need to feel it! What are

your senses telling you? When you consider a decision, does your breathing change, do you feel sick, does your heart beat faster, are your muscles tense? Focus on your dilemma and calm yourself down. Breathe steadily, close your eyes, sit quietly, and recognise the chatter in your brain and the nerves in your body. When you're feeling relaxed, gently question if the unsureness comes from social or familial expectations, and can therefore be ignored, or from your best self. Does your gut reaction to a question or dilemma reflect your true values? If so, can you act upon it?

3 **When you've gone through the logical and the visceral, combine the two** and speak your truth. Tell your gut of your decision, and sit with it. Do you feel a sense of calm, or do you feel stressed? If you've done the right thing, you might feel drained and exhausted, but you should feel settled. You still have the drama and difficulty of executing your decision, but at least you know you have come at it from a place that works for you.

Learning this 1–2–3 approach to trusting your gut will help you in all areas of your life – from deciding if you really need that second bar of chocolate (sometimes you really do), to welcoming a new friend into your inner circle. Today, I stop, listen, think and feel through most things – not in some take-myself-off-to-a-cabin-in-the-woods-and-contemplate way, but in a quick flash of head and heart that combines to give off vibes. I love good vibes.

I still get it wrong and beat myself up about it, but I have the tools to know how to recover and learn from it. And if you really can't trust yourself, get yourself a trustworthy friend or family member who has only your best interests at heart. He or she can act as your conscience and guide. Trust yourself to recognise this person when you find them.

Getting real: Solveig, 45

'I am a sentimentalist in every area of my life. I feel the moments as they change from the present into the past, and how memory lives in the way in which we sometimes clutter our lives with emotional and material things. It's the opposite of simplicity – in particular Marie Condo's brand of simple. But there is, I think, duplicity in simplicity. Our things and our choices are also a form of autobiography, and if they are oversimplified I'm not sure what one is left with. Clearing one's mind can mean different things to different people. For me, this year, I'm channelling Spike Lee and always considering how to "do the right thing". My other method is to paraphrase Aristotle, and remember it's what you do every day when you're down in the mess of it all that matters. The power to persevere – not what you do here and there, when life is easy or great – but what you do in the dull moments, the uneasy moments, is what matters.'

How to become your own muse

It can be invaluable to recognise and observe smart, kind people and edit their best qualities into your life and learn from them, but it is equally important to take an honest look at your own skills, attributes and talents, build on them, and give yourself the admiration and respect you deserve. We all need a mentor, but we all need to be our own muse, too. How?

Work hard, stay humble When I suggest you become your own muse, I'm not suggesting you become an egotistical maniac. I'd like you to be realistic and kind to yourself as you begin your journey to self-musedom. Humility will allow you to survey your strong points without falling into the trap of thinking that you always know best and cannot learn anything new. Accept that you need work on some areas.

Build ritual and routine As you move to becoming your own muse, make time in your day to note events, interactions or ideas that have come your way and can be built into something meaningful. Keep a journal or gratitude diary, or build a reflective time for meditation into your morning routine or bedtime wind-down.

Dismiss structures that work for other people, but don't work for you. Know your truth and stop caring if someone else thinks that your way of working or thinking is silly, strange or sucks. Give yourself permission to trust your gut and listen to your heart.

Keep it simple As you slowly become your own muse, start with one true thing: I base my actions in kindness always; I set limits to protect myself and my family; I can say no to things that don't serve me and yes to things that will help me to grow (and I can determine which is which). A personal mantra, repeated and lived, is a great place to start.

Be passionate about your life Or at least one aspect of it to start with. If you want to start a new hobby, get fit, read more, be your own muse in that one area of your life, giving yourself the mental space to fulfil that dream, the physical time to make it happen, the self-confidence to know it can be achieved. Your best self is your best muse.

Find a space that allows the growth you desire This may be in a book club, or in a gym that offers classes, or within a professional networking group. Give yourself the tools to revolve, ruminate and contemplate your inner strengths and workings.

Search for meaning in everyday life Artists look to their muse for this, but you can find it within yourself. Be curious about your own life and how it could be best lived, constantly and judiciously changing things that aren't fulfilling your needs. Be responsible for yourself and your own happiness and never stop looking for ways to be better.

Be democratic Don't become a dictator, shutting out the thoughts and opinions offered by people you trust and admire, or ignoring a warning bell ringing in your head or a butterfly wriggling in your tummy. Always be open to inspiration from those around you. Listen to and value what others have to say, digest it, and extract the beneficial.

Stay active Give yourself the best chance of being happy and healthy. Collect inspirational quotes and images, notice how people you respect have become their own muse and borrow elements that would work for you; capture energy and formulas to keep in reserve for the minutes, hours, days and years that leave you drained, fretful or unsure of your own possibility or power.

The salve in solitude

Being a social butterfly and a party animal is good, but sometimes being alone with your thoughts and ideas – especially when coupled with the soul-enlivening, mind-expanding bloom of forests, lakes, mountains and oceans – is invaluable. Solitude is not the same as loneliness. Solitude is not a negative state. Looking for it does not mean that you are depressed, antisocial or sad, it means you are self-aware enough to know that you need a break from the constant claxons of commuting, children's chatter, cyberspace and that internal voice telling us that we're wrong or bad, or could do better. We are overstimulated and overwrought, overstretched and overanxious. Alonetime, in a location that makes us feel calm and nurtured, can soothe, replenish and rejuvenate. You need to swap your FOMO (fear of missing out) for the double whammy boost of JOMO (joy of missing out) and JONO (joy of no). You can turn down invitations (punctually and politely) if you need time to yourself.

How to politely turn down a golden ticket

- It's an invitation, not an instruction. Don't feel guilty for safeguarding your diary.
- Don't ignore it. The host won't be offended if you can't attend, but it will be offensive if you allow the host to accommodate you but then don't show up or don't get back to them. Respect their budget, time frame and space.
- Don't make up a lie – you could catch yourself out. Less is more, you don't need to give a long-winded, exaggerated dramatic excuse. You are allowed to simply say, 'I'm sorry but I can't this time.' If you go on too much, it'll sound like you're making excuses.
- Always say 'Thanks for including me.' It's polite and to the point. Add 'Do please ask me again' – but only if you mean it!
- If the invite was for a big event such as a fortieth birthday party or a wedding, do send a card or gift if you can. And if it is someone you're fond of, do follow up with a message asking how the event went and how you'd love to see them soon – again, only if you genuinely mean it!

The power of one

There are physical and psychological reasons to prioritise alone time and say goodbye to anxiety, burnout and exhaustion:

- Being constantly switched on and at the whim of others doesn't give the brain time to unwind. Being by yourself without constant distractions, however, gives your mind the chance to unravel everything and relax.
- Travelling alone or starting a new hobby *tout seul* can actually help you to, in the long run, meet more like-minded people. If you try these things in an already established group, you are less likely to be open to new people and new friends. Trying new things alone pushes you out of comfort zones and the uncomfortable patterns and established routines that may have been forcing you into a stereotype or expected role.
- Taking on a new challenge? Concentration improves without interruptions, and your productivity will go up, too. You don't need a gang to sign up with you to embark on a new hobby.
- When you spend time alone, you get to silence the voices around you and to think and decide for yourself who, what and where you want to be. You make time for others. Give yourself the same courtesy.
- We all have an introverted side, however much we try to hide it, and alone time will refill our cup of

sociality so that we can communicate better over the course of the following day or week.

- The never-ending whirl of chatter and movement prevents you from thinking deeply and creatively. Be still and let the new emotions and ideas flow. Solitude is the perfect state for specific problem solving.

- Hanging out with yourself is actually less stressful and can be just as fun as hanging out with others. You want to explore a city park and you want to do it now, so go – why wait for others to fit you into their diary and then let you down at the last minute? Be your own wingman. That way you get to do exactly what you want to do.

- Being alone in nature will allow you to reconnect deeply with the living world around you without feeling the social pressure to make small talk. Reconnecting to nature far from the madding crowd will allow you to stimulate your senses more powerfully – you'll hear birdsong, feel the wind, and so on – giving you time to embrace the feelings of awe and gratitude that Mother Nature provokes. You'll also get a boost in bravery, peacefulness and determination.

- Taking time on your own could stop you from feeling lonely, because the more time you spend getting to know yourself and what you want, the easier it will be to truly understand who you want around you and why – and that those who don't give you the warm and fuzzies don't deserve any of your time.

Getting real: Laura, 40

'In terms of life editing and selfishly protecting my own boundaries and health, I've found it helpful to think of it more in terms of what I say *yes* to, as opposed to what I say *no* to. I have a finite amount of energy in any given day. How do I want to spend it? Where do I want to place it? I do think it's helpful to think of it as energy and not as time, because everyone says ten times a day, "I don't have time", and it hardly even means anything any more. But if I think: *Right, it's not time, it's energy,* and I think of it like a budget, I get to decide how to use it, whereas time feels out of my hands. This helps me (at least on a good day) to more mindfully connect to my priorities in life. It's easier to say, "Yes, this is important to me and so I want to devote time and energy to it" rather than feeling that I'm constantly saying no to things.'

You are enough, so that's enough

Stop bullying yourself into being more, doing more, wanting more ... or criticising yourself for not being where you thought you should be, or where your friends are. Treat yourself gently.

We are trained to diminish our accomplishments, refuse compliments, look for faults and over-share failings, and, over time, this incessant banter can really hit our self-worth. I'm not suggesting you become an insufferable egomaniac or know-it-all, but I *am* suggesting that you edit out your negative inner voice and replace it with a more decent one. If you talk or think of yourself badly, it gives others permission to do the same, so you need to cut it out – especially if you're a parent. Retrain how you speak to yourself – inwardly and in public.

Say this, not that!

Remember that so much of how we talk to ourselves is based on feelings *not* facts, and they are not based on reality or how others see us. Check your emotions when you're practising negative self-talk, and balance your bad vibes with some good ones:

- Say, 'I feel like I'm not good enough right now', and not 'I am not good enough.'
- Say, 'I'll never run a marathon, but I'm a great dancer', and not 'I can't run.'
- Say, 'This is hard, but this is a fresh start', and not 'I failed once, I'll fail again.'
- Say, 'Everyone makes mistakes, I'll learn from this', and not 'I'm always making mistakes. What is wrong with me?'

Set some boundaries on your own brain If your mind starts scrambling to a place of can't, won't or don't, call it out. Why is your inner critic putting you down? Be honest with yourself, assess the safety aspects of each pursuit, gag your inner critic, and go ahead if a decision really is right for you. Again, trust your gut, not the Negative Nelly character who's been lurking in your hippocampus since you were a child. Silence the drama.

Enjoy your successes – and acknowledge your defeats – with an honest appraisal of what you could do differently next time to create the best story for you. Don't let past failures lurk in dark, lonely places – bring them out into the open so that your inner critic can't sneak up on you with cruel whispers. Accept that you can't always win but that often it's the failing that teaches you the most and the subsequent successes that give you the most pleasure.

If the voice in your head is too persistently negative, talk to someone who you trust cares about you. Your inner critic distorts reality; an outsider can be honest but fair. Hire a professional. There is no shame in editing your life with the help of a therapist or life coach.

Cut something out of your daily routine to make time for you to keep an accomplishment journal. List all the things you've done – big and small – that make you proud. Read it and refer to it when you're suffering a self-esteem tumble. Finishing a novel, volunteering at a local charity, going to the gym, doing a favour for a friend or getting enough sleep – note down all these things. As the list grows, so will your inner confidence.

Know that you're not alone Everyone has moments where something inside them is telling them that they are not enough. Even the friend who looks perfect, who you aspire to grow into, who you jealously get yourself into a funk about when you're at your lowest. Be the trusted confidant who helps silence other people's inner critic. Being thoughtful and kind are two things that you should never cut back on.

Getting real: Isabella, 30

'I am not terribly materialistic when it comes to clothes, handbags or shoes, but I have to constantly fight house envy. I attend lots of functions in gorgeous homes and, for a while, before I defined what my issue was, I'd leave each party in a disgruntled mood, snapping at my boyfriend and feeling sorry for myself. I have tried to reframe my own thoughts of house envy to being happy for my friend to live in such a beautiful space; it feels so much better. Instead of hiding my jealousy, I express it. "How lovely your home is! I'd love to live here," I admit to the host, instead of doing my old, unhealthy bottling up.'

Diplomatic immunity

We need to speak truth to power, but we still need to be fair, balanced and polite. Diplomacy is a skill, and one worth learn-ing. It is always better to respond to criticism or judgement than to react to it – even if every bone in your body is yelling 'This is bullshit!' Can you do you, without offending anyone? Yes, with a few etiquette reminders:

- Act with decorum. Channel Michelle Obama and her 'when they go low, we go high' vibes. Your dignity should give you some comfort when dealing with people who are not as authentically evolved as you.
- Ask questions rather than shouting answers. You know your thoughts and feelings; perhaps you could learn something from people with opposing views. Treat every conversation with a difficult or challenging person as a social study. Looking at insulting exchanges like this had helped me not to cry, not to feel injured, and stopped me walking away. Share your opinions, and let others speak.
- Respect differences. Your truth is not everyone's truth. People are born and raised differently. Engage your brain. You can probably work out on a gut level if someone is being spiteful or just doesn't agree with you. Differing opinions are allowed. Imagine walking in another person's shoes.
- Avoid people. If one person repeatedly gets your hackles up, and you are not forced through work or living next door to each other to communicate, step away. Send good wishes for them out into the world and admit that you're just not each other's kind of person. If the negatives from your interactions outweigh the positives, move on. Resentment and dread are two emotions that you should cut from your new edited life as much as possible.
- If you go too far in your new gung-ho truth-seeking zest for life, and you fear – or hear – that you have hurt someone's feelings, apologise. You're not backing

down, but you're acknowledging that you made someone feel bad, and guilt is another heavy emotion that you don't need in your streamlined life. Learn from it and adapt your future behaviour accordingly.

Own your story – here's how

It's time to check in and note, score and plan your most authentic life going forward. In this chapter we've covered who you should look up to, and how you should value yourself more. Reflect on this by asking yourself these questions.

*A*nalyse your happiness
How can you be more joyful?

U pgrade your habits
What traits should you ditch for a healthier life?

T reat yourself kindly
Are you practising self-care?

H ave faith in your core values
Are you keeping to your principles?

E xpand your horizons
What do you need more of? What would make your heart or mind grow?

N arrow down negative influences
Is someone making you doubt yourself? Do you need to continue this relationship?   ▶

*T*ake time to improve your skills
What could you learn this year?

*I*mprove your thinking
Are you coming from a place of wisdom and strength?

*C*ut back on pursuits that clutter
What should you trim from daily life?

Chapter 3

Healthy is Your Happy Place

'Health is the greatest possession. Contentment is the
greatest treasure. Confidence is the greatest friend.
Non-being is the greatest joy.'

Lao Tzu

Without good health, we have nothing. We appreciate this in the
instant we hear the sad news of someone's death or of a heartbreaking diagnosis; life is now a fight, every step a dare, every
breath a challenge. When we lose a loved one – or even someone
in the public eye who we admired – we wonder how they faced
the end. Was it with annoyance that they didn't change things
before it was too late? Did their life's mistakes flash before them?
The physical blunders we know about, such as smoking tobacco,
drinking too much and moving too little, and the mental mis-
calculations: taking on too much, worrying about everything,
making bad choices about who we spend our time with, and
saying yes to work over play?

In her groundbreaking book *The Top Five Regrets of the Dying: A*

Life Transformed by the Dearly Departing, palliative nurse Bronnie Ware found there was a general consensus from the hundreds of patients she cared for in their last three months, five regrets that were repeated:

1. Not having the courage to live the life they truly wanted, but the life others expected of them.
2. Working too much and missing out on family milestones.
3. Not having the courage to express their true feelings.
4. Not staying in touch with friends.
5. Not allowing themselves to just be happy.

We read these truths, and we acknowledge their authenticity – we can imagine feeling the same way. And when sad, shocking news stops us in our tracks, we are reminded of them, but quickly, too easily perhaps, the shock, grief and fear subside, our regular routines pick up, and our focus shifts back to the stuff that doesn't matter: the size of our bottoms, the traffic, a spotty chin, a funny look from a stranger in a coffee shop. I'm not suggesting that we wander around in a morbid gloom, but a little less focus on things we won't even remember in a week's time should be one of the first things we edit out to make space to appreciate the blessings we have. Especially when it comes to good health.

Death wish

Twelve months ago, I was co-chairing a school fundraiser, which took a lot of time, energy and commitment from all us parents planning it. We were volunteers, putting our time in for free to raise enough money to pay the salaries for the reading and maths specialists, and the technology teacher, and although the event should have been awash in goodwill and gratitude, a few non-helpers were moaning about the date, the theme – anything and everything. On the day of the party, as I was driving to the venue to start setting up, a message flashed up on my phone: a dear friend and ex-colleague of mine from my New York maga-zine days had finally succumbed to the brain cancer she'd been courageously battling for two years. I fell apart in the traffic jam, drowning in flashbacks of photo shoots, planning meetings and office karaoke parties. Pulling up at my destination, I had to force myself to stop crying, dry my face and mentally prepare for the 15-hour shift of cleaning, decorating, hosting and guid-ing caterers and DJs.

It wasn't long before mean-spirited comments found their way to my hard-working crew – complaints about the start time, seating, and so on – and upsetting them. It was all so petty and pointless, and filled with this grief-stricken tiger blood I felt for the loss of my friend, I wouldn't stand for it, and so I roared. 'Don't let anyone upset you. You are working hard, for free, with one intention: to raise money for our school. If anyone has any-thing rude to say, or an insignificant grumble, send them to me. My friend died this morning. She was 44 and she would do any-thing to be attending a party tonight.' That shut the moaners up immediately, I can tell you, and of course, as I grieved for her over the following months, her passing made me reassess how I handled my own stress and irritations, and the ridiculousness of letting insignificant or silly things negatively and pointlessly affect my health.

An authenticity edit – to create a life that you love – must include acknowledging that some displeasures can niggle but should not consume you, and that one cannot lose sight of what is really worth bitching about. I've lost three good friends in the last couple of years – two to cancer, one to depression, all in their thirties or forties. Good health is too important to treat foolishly. Value it.

How to manage your physical health

Some people are programmed with an inner drive towards good health and fitness. I envy those exemplary human beings. My ideal exercise plan – one that I could stick to – would involve less ab crunching and more crunching of Ferrero Rocher wrappers, and less running and more running-man dance moves to 'Shake Your Thang' by Salt-N-Pepa during an at-home disco with my kids. My natural habitat is sitting on a sofa with a pile of books and a cup of coffee, not getting sweaty among muscle-bods at a CrossFit Studio. But, I have to self-motivate because I like my life and want to keep living it, and I also appreciate that physical wellness boosts my mental wellness, which is always important but now more so than ever as I tiptoe towards the panicky, sweaty, moody and achy precipice of menopause during this unprecedented time in our shared history. I eat better, drink less alcohol and move more than I ever have before, and I have made these edits for my happiest self and for my children. As the Buddha wisely noted, 'to keep the body in good health is a duty ... otherwise we shall not be able to keep our mind strong and clear'.

Body maths

The body is miraculously self-healing and regenerative. If we cut back on negative influences or add some positive ones, we reap benefits within days, weeks – and sometimes minutes! Use this knowledge to boost your willpower and become the changed person you want to be.

Subtractions

When you stop smoking after just one hour your heart rate returns to normal, your blood pressure drops and your circulation should begin to improve. After one day the noxious carbon monoxide inhaled from cigarettes gets out of your body and the level of oxygen in your system increases. In just 24 hours without a smoke, your chance of suffering a heart attack or heart disease lessens. After two days, your senses will improve – life will literally smell and taste better. For the following three months, it's all good news, as your lung function and circulation continue to improve. The golden ticket is at the ten-year mark, when the body has healed the damage you've done and your chance of having a stroke, or getting lung, mouth, throat or pancreatic cancer, is significantly reduced. After 20 years smoke-free, you're back to where you started: your risk of dying from smoking-related causes is the same as someone who has never smoked in their life.

When you stop drinking the body spends the first 24 hours after your last drink working hard to get the alcohol out of your system. It is a toxin, remember. Within your first wine-free week, you'll start sleeping more deeply, which will boost your mental and physical energy, your skin will be more hydrated so it will look younger, and uncomfortable conditions such as eczema and rosacea might improve. Research shows that after a week without booze, people make better food choices, leading to healthy weight loss too. After two weeks, sleep and skin continue to get better and better. Your stomach lining returns to normal, and, if you suffer from acid reflux, that should resolve. Within a month of stopping drinking, you have better kidney health, improved vision and you've reduced your risk of a stroke or heart issues. You've also reduced your liver fat by up to 15 per cent, which boosts your body's ability to store vitamins and minerals. After three months of non-drinking, you will have reduced your chances of getting cancer and, a huge plus, the one I've noticed in friends after they've joined AA or chosen to be teetotal for health reasons, your mood, productivity and focus improve. You can't see the internal changes of sober living, but the external ones are splendidly hard to ignore.

When you stop drinking fizzy drinks positive benefits are immediate and long term. If you switch to water, you'll be more hydrated. Fizzy sodas often contain caffeine, a diuretic, which puts a strain on your kidneys. Cutting out these drinks will help you to avoid tooth decay and discoloured enamel, and it'll also reduce your calorie and sugar intake, which will help your metabolism and blood pressure – and it lowers your diabetes risk. And don't think that if you are addicted to *diet* sodas, you're getting away with anything. One study of 2,500 people who drank diet fizzy drinks showed that they had a 61 per cent higher incidence of stroke and heart disease than those who preferred the non-fizzy versions.

When you stop, or cut back on, eating red meat, which is calorie-dense, it can help you to lose a few pounds. Research in the *Journal of General Internal Medicine* showed how people on a vegetarian diet lost more weight than those still eating meat, and vegans shed even more. It's worth considering if you do need to make healthy weight-loss choices. Red meat is also highly acidic, which knocks the body's balance off kilter. As your body digests red meat more slowly than other foods, it can promote bloating, constipation and gas – all things we'd like less of. Fibre-rich whole foods will reduce these issues and build healthy bacteria in the gut to lower body-wide inflammation. Trimming down – or trimming out – red meat will decrease the amount of saturated fats you're consuming, helping to lower your cholesterol and potentially reduce your chances of getting colon or bowel cancer. In 2015, the World Health Organization classified red meat as a possible carcinogen. Processed red meats such as sausages are also full of nitrates, which are believed to be another contributor to some cancers. And outside of yourself, think about the planet. A substantial percentage of the world's greenhouse gas emissions are caused by animal agriculture, according to a study undertaken by the Worldwatch Institute. Perhaps think about committing to a weekly Meatless Monday, and when you do eat meat, opt for high-quality, organic produce from sustainably farmed animals.

Getting real: Kirsty, 50

'Two years ago, I was diagnosed with chronic lympho-
cytic leukaemia (CLL), a blood cancer. The tiredness,
headaches, night sweats and UTIs – which I'd put down
to being a busy working mum in my forties – had an
explanation. On the day I was diagnosed, my ten-year-
old daughter was in the car with my dad and asked, "Is
Mummy going to die?" He reassured her that I wouldn't,
but in truth no one really knew. Luckily, I found a donor,
underwent a successful stem-cell transfer and six
months later I regained my physical strength, and found
a remarkable mental strength, too. Along with his DNA,
my donor gave me a new outlook. Before my diagnosis,
I lived life at breakneck speed and felt the need to control everything. Today, I don't get stressed. I don't fall
out with people or fight. His gift – and my gift to myself
post-cancer – is that I have let go of my own expectations and external pressures. Life really is too short.'

Additions

When you start exercising, within ten minutes, your body is on
your side and making it easier for you to get fit. Your heart rate
increases, boosting the supply of blood to your brain, making
you more alert, blocking pain signals and increasing the feel-
good endorphins rushing through your system. For 72 hours
after exercise, your metabolic rate is raised, helping you to burn
calories. After a week, studies show, positive physiological and

psychological changes are happening. Self-confidence lifts while depression lessens. After a month of regular, sensible exercise – I'm not talking marathons – you can expect to see good changes, such as improved productivity (you have a spring in your step), a reduction in sick days and ailments, and you'll feel happier across all areas of your life.

When you start drinking enough water you'll feel flushed with good luck – because staying hydrated literally flushes out toxins, keeping your bowels moving as they should, removing waste from your kidneys (needed to avoid kidney stones and UTIs) and making your joints glide better. Being dehydrated, especially when you're overheated, can make you feel dizzy, light-headed and confused, so drinking enough stops those nasty side effects. Your intellect sharpens – remember, your brain is 75 per cent water, so a hydrated noggin is needed. Introducing extra water to your day replaces the empty sugary calories you consume when you think you're hungry, but you're actually just dehydrated, which can help you control overeating and lose weight. Is there a perfect amount of H_2O to get all this good stuff? Current recommendations are approximately 15 cups per day for men and 11 cups per day for women.

When you start eating more fruit and vegetables you'll glow, as they're loaded with vitamins A, C and E – all known to fight blemish-building free radicals and promote radiance. The phytonutrients and high water content reduce wrinkles and crow's feet and improve the skin's texture. Red and orange veggies containing beta-carotene protect your skin from sun damage. Fresh, frozen, dried or canned – eat the rainbow and eat it daily. Your digestive system will work more efficiently, making you poop more regularly, therefore flattening your tummy. But, away from the aesthetics, researchers at Imperial College London discovered that if everyone were to eat ten servings of fruit and veg daily, 7.8 million premature deaths worldwide would be prevented. Upping our green and leafy intake might help in the prevention of stroke, cancer and heart disease. Let's take the vitamins one by one: vitamin A keeps your eyes and skin healthy and wards off infections, B reduces depression and anxiety, C keeps your gums healthy and helps wounds heal, while D is essential for bone health and good muscle function. Vitamin K is very important, too: K1 from vegetables; K2 from animal foods, butter. And if you're pregnant, or trying to be, increase your folic acid to help with healthy foetal development.

Journal your journey – losses and gains

Exercise your mind by listing three subtractions that you should or could make from your lifestyle, and then list three additions that could boost your body. Write or type them into your daily calendar to remind yourself of your commitment until they become routine.

Walk, don't run!

As with all major life changes – even the healthy ones – we need to practise due diligence, so instead of blindly following a trend, test if it really is good for *you*. With any new regime, don't run before you can walk. And perhaps never run – perhaps just focus on walking. A few years ago, both my brothers ran the London Marathon, raising money for very worthy causes and boosting their mental and physical health no end. Inspired, I dug out my trainers and started to jog a little, a few times a week. The psychological lift I got from it was amazing – I felt powerful and lighter, but sadly my knees didn't agree. One blew up like a balloon and the other wobbled and creaked like a dilapidated rocking chair. I followed all the correct advice: warming up before and stretching after, buying the correct trainers and, yes, even running socks, and not pushing myself. Still I had no joy, so instead I embraced the simple delights of walking – or hiking, as the Hollywood crowd like to call it – and I have been happy to see benefits and a calorie burn very similar to my hobbling runs. Yes, to get a similar effect to a 30-minute run now takes me a chunkier hour, but I've accepted my legit limitations. And a study of inactive women who began low-impact exercise for just 75 minutes per week showed that they improved their fitness levels significantly over those in the test group who continued doing nothing. If you run without damaging yourself, brilliant. If you can't, switch it up and walk the walk. There are many reasons we should edit more brisk walking into our lives:

- It's super-social with no huffing and puffing, just good conversation if you choose to partner up with someone. Call it quality time with your mum, your daughter, your friend who needs to talk about something serious, or your colleague with a hangover. Look for self-guided nature walks in local gardens or historic houses and ask neighbours if they'd be interested in starting a walking group.

- It's free and doesn't require any special equipment or time frame – it can be done at any time of day, in any season.
- It's a more efficient exercise than we give it credit for. Just 30 minutes of walking per day increases muscle power, endurance and cardiovascular fitness, reduces excess body fat, strengthens bones, boosts balance and reduces your chance of developing conditions such as osteoporosis and heart disease.
- Walking won't produce the serious injuries associated with more vigorous fitness regimes. It is a weight-bearing exercise (that is, you carry your own weight) so it increases your cardiovascular and lung fitness, but it's unlikely that you'll twist a nerve, pull a muscle or tear a ligament. To get the benefits, walk at a speed that means you're still be able to talk, but not sing!
- Not everyone loves wearing a pedometer but as a rule-follower who loves ticking off achievements, I'll wear one when I'm feeling unmotivated – to give me a confidence upswing when I hit my 10,000 steps. The number might be arbitrary, but it focuses my attention in the right direction.
- When you're really walking the walk, add appropriate hand weights, go for longer, try more hills or speed up.

Strokes of luck: why we should edit more swimming into our lives

Swimming is the best thing to ever crawl into my marriage. Impressed by a sprightly, 85-year-old neighbour, my husband asked how he always looked so good and seemed so calm. 'I swim,' he revealed – and that was that. Now, every morning at 5am, whatever the weather, my husband slips out of bed and heads to our local pool to swim a mile, his middle-age crisis, weird stuff and stress sinking to the bottom, never to be seen again. He's never had an injury, and is noticeably nicer for adding it to his routine.

Swimming is the ideal way to exercise for all fitness levels and ages because it is gentle on joints, gives your heart and lungs a great aerobic workout, and the water resistance builds muscle and lowers blood pressure. You can burn the most calories doing fast crawl or butterfly stroke, but any stroke will offer a good, all-round body workout. Swimming in warm water has been proven to ease stiffness and pain and increase flexibility by reducing the load on joints, which is specifically useful for pregnant women, the overweight or those with arthritis. Hydrotherapy, as swimming or floating in water is known, also has a calming effect on the mind; the weightlessness of water offering a physical and mental distraction from the weight of life's worries. The breathing patterns that you fall into during a swim regulate brain waves, which also quieten the interior chatter that leads to anxiety. Swimming in the sea has its own name, it's that special: thalassotherapy (a word first used by the god of all things good for us, Hippocrates, no less). Ocean water is rich in minerals including sodium, chloride, sulphate, calcium and magnesium – all helpful healers of skin conditions such as psoriasis and eczema. Ocean swimming is also known to reduce the symptoms of hay fever and respiratory issues. One reason suggested is that the saline reduces inflammation in the nose and throat. Seawater is also brimming with microorganisms that produce antibiotic and antibacterial immunity boosters in humans, so, let's ride this wellness wave, shall we?

Getting real: Anna, 35

'This time last year I had a total burnout. My body was sore, my mind was jumbled and I wasn't coping at all. Trying to balance work with raising a family felt impossible, like I was spinning far too many plates. They started to crash to the floor one by one and my panic and anxiety rose. Everything was too much. Sensing my stress, my cousin suggested we meet for a hike and a swim along the coast in Scotland, near to where we both lived. It felt like a very decadent thing to do, taking that time out when everything was so busy, but I knew I needed this like oxygen. When we arrived to face the blue – the huge expanse of beach was ours alone – it was so cold that we could see our breath. I was nervous but I reminded myself that I needed a release. As I fought my way in, I roared at the waves as they battered me one after the other. I just let it all out – the worries, the sadness, the doubts – into the ocean. Before long, the tears and frustration became huge belly laughs and we played in the water like little children.'

Seven ways . . .

. . . that physical pursuits can help you to live a life you love.

When I talked about health with my good friend Anna Deacon, who, along with co-author Vicky Allan, wrote *Taking the Plunge: The Healing Power of Wild Swimming for Mind, Body & Soul*, she described the many ways that wild swimming had brought about the mental wellness she needed, with the social and mental aspects being as beneficial as the body boost. I have found this, too, in my daily walking routine, and in my once-a-week Pilates class, with a good friend instructing me while another encourages me. I know other friends have experienced this too, through joining a dance class or yoga group.

1. **Mindfulness** It is impossible to swim outdoors in the cold, hike uphill or do a sun salutation while thinking about anything other than exactly what you are doing at that moment.
2. **Pain relief** Stretching, moving, being plunged into freezing water or working up a sweat are natural ways to ease away aches.
3. **Depression** All exercise, from the lightest to the most intensive, can help manage the symptoms of depression and anxiety.
4. **Stress** When you train your body to handle shock, pain and discomfort through repeated exercise, it can deal with smaller stresses more easily.   ▶

5. **Community** Find your fitness friendship group for support. These people will prove to be advocates for you in the moment, during training, and in other aspects of your life.

6. **Body confidence** When you push your body, or work with it, or allow it to move and stretch, you feel proud and your body and mind find their purpose. The results of this will last way beyond the half-hour while you're practising.

7. **Glee** Think of children at the beach, in the forest: running, swinging, swimming, leaping, jumping. This can be us, too, if we just allow ourselves to be free, moving towards bliss.

How to manage pain

Six years ago, I got my first migraine. I'd given birth to my daughter six weeks previously and my hormones were a mess, I hadn't slept properly for as long as I could remember, and my body was exhausted. As a dark thunder swept across my head, I remember clutching my baby to my chest not understanding what was happening. I managed to get her safely into her crib before I vomited, the axes and lightning rods of pain chipping away at the right side of my skull from eye socket to jaw, then I passed out on the bathroom floor. These episodes became a regular occurrence from then on. They always started the same way: a heavy cloud clunking down on my brow, a chill in my bones so deep I'd start to shiver, a dizziness that brought nausea, and then the pain: my brain ripped up and yanked through my right ear. In the grip of this torture – which tended to last for 72 hours every couple of weeks – the pain was so bad that if it wasn't for my children, I confessed to my husband, I'd have chosen to take a pill and never wake up. This was my first authentic moment around discussing my health.

At first, I was ashamed to admit my frailty, but discussions with fellow chronic pain sufferers told me that if we didn't speak up honestly about how it affected our lives, society's views would never become kinder. 'I've been accused of acting or exaggerating my pain,' a friend with severe lower back pain told me during my time of personal despair. 'And I fought back and said, "No, I'm *acting* when I attend an event and smile, or converse, or get myself to my desk to work. I'm *pretending* to be normal when inside all I can think about is the agony."' A 2019 survey of 6,000 people by the University of Toronto revealed that migraine sufferers are twice as likely to be depressed and have suicidal thoughts as non-sufferers. This reminded me just how important it is not only to make life edits to increase your chance of wellness and relief, but also to have authentic conversations about pain so that sufferers feel less alone and misunderstood.

Once I realised that my migraines weren't going away, I turned to my doctor. A year of MRI scans, urine samples and blood tests proved that there was nothing wrong with me, just fluctuating hormones around my cycle and a mother's sleep deprivation. What was I told to do: add things, ask for more opinions, bring in more stuff – medicine, treatments, worry? First, I was handed a prescription for Sumatriptan and basically told 'bad luck, get on with it'. Drugged, the migraines, though lessened, became longer – and fellow migraine sufferers told me that Sumatriptan gave them hangovers, and they'd benefited from binning the medication. I stopped that and my doctor, focusing on the rollercoaster ride of my hormones, put me on a three-month contraceptive pill commonly prescribed to women with menstrual migraine. The philosophy was that a steadying of my cycle, removing the dramatic oestrogen highs and lows would quieten the root cause of my pain. I bled heavily for 10 of the 12 weeks, gained 4.5kg (10lb), felt lethargic *and* still endured my usual headaches. I threw my next three-month prescription away, too. Back to prescription painkillers, and this time Topiramate. I had a new doctor by now, who warned me that despite people getting great results, it had the tendency to dull the intellect. I thought she was exaggerating until, a month in, I looked at my laptop and couldn't remember how to type – which isn't great for a writer – and knew I couldn't take them any longer. I worried there was nothing for it but to go back to dosing myself up with Ibuprofen, which gave me the horrid side effect of stomach cramps, and wishing my days away.

Keep calm and cut stuff out

Until, that was, in a lucid period of well-being just over a year ago, it dawned on me that I needed to become my own health-care advocate and turn away from pharmaceuticals and look deeper into my lifestyle. I'd been aware of friends with arthritis, fibromyalgia and depression doing the same with great success. What triggered me? I needed to get to the root cause ... and instead of *adding* things, perhaps I needed to do a lifestyle edit and cut things *out*?

My diet was the first thing I looked at. I knew that I felt extrafuzzy-headed and gloomy after alcohol and that I should cut back. As a depressant and toxin, booze isn't the best wellness asset for anyone, but it made me feel particularly wretched, with hangovers and headaches intermingling. Going cold turkey, I then turned to nutritionist Kate Llewellyn-Waters, who fine-tunes her What If Plan to her patients using DNA analysis, and I took a saliva test. 'It is important for you to reduce your exposure to dietary and environmental pro-carcinogens such as smoking, amines and nitrates, which could cause reactions such as headaches, and to increase detoxifying vegetables such as broccoli, kale and garlic, which edit out oxidative stress,' she told me. On her advice, for the last year I have been careful to eat a more whole-food-based diet, cutting out triggers. I also cut back on my beloved coffee: two cups of coffee before midday, and no more. This life edit improved my quality of sleep. It's a must for everyone – especially people dealing with chronic pain.

It is probably the rituals of self-care, however, that have been most effective in reducing my symptoms, prompted by a frank conversation with my friend MeriJayd O'Connor, a craniosacral therapist who specialises in chronic pain relief. 'When it comes to chronic pain, there's no one-size-fits-all cure. Each person has a unique set of conditions inside the body and life situations that can manifest themselves as illness, pain and disorders. It is important to look at diet, stress and coping habits, then to dive deeper into the body to look at what needs to function better. The body remembers everything that we have done to it and has to compensate or use energy to work around it. During times of panic, hormonal imbalance or poor diet, the body says "Enough!", which can bring on experiences such as migraines.'

This made so much sense. The stress and sleeplessness of trying to balance motherhood and work had caused my migraines, I was sure.

I did lie down in MeriJayd's treatment room, and she gently touched my limbs, manipulated my joints and soothed my muscles, but it was on my psyche that she had done the most work. She had reminded me of the huge impact of stress on the body, and how self-care isn't a fad or a luxury but has a very real health benefit. I had to slow down, do what I had to and say no to the extras that led me to feel anxious or overburdened. The same week I spoke to MeriJayd, a different friend suggested that I keep a wellness notebook, writing down migraine days and what I'd done to look after myself – or not – in the lead up to the episode. I started writing a detailed account of my weeks, such as changing emotions – teary, angry – and physical aches and pains, and this simple ritual reminded me that I mattered more than keeping up with the Joneses or a bustling social life.

The last 12 months have taught me that honesty about pain, self-kindness and self-awareness – and stopping saying yes because you think you *should* – are key to managing my migraines. I prepare myself for an episode. If a fog starts to descend across the right side of my head, I unplug all unnecessary technology and avoid social media, because it can make me feel negative and anxious, and it saps me of energy that I don't have to give. I say no to any extracurricular activities that aren't crucial to me or my children's welfare. I force myself to have early, uniform bedtimes and to get eight hours of sleep instead of showing up to events that I don't have the energy or true desire to join. I don't beat myself up if the laundry piles up for a few days, or if I take an afternoon nap. I eat and hydrate regularly.

These rituals are not just beneficial to chronic pain sufferers, they are simple, healthy rituals that can benefit us all and keep adrenal fatigue the utter exhaustion that too often rides alongside us on our drive for perfection, at bay.

Getting real: Hayley, 45

'I had a "funny turn" earlier this year. It had all the symptoms of a stroke: one half of my face collapsed, my tongue rolled out and my speech was slurred (all witnessed by my poor 15-year-old). It only lasted for about 30 seconds and I felt as if I was underwater for the duration. I hadn't realised quite how stressed I had been over the previous months: working, studying at university, essay deadlines, builders in the house 24/7 and dealing with stresses that the children had at school. I thought I'd had a stroke and so everything went on hold. I stayed in bed, rested and put my health first instead of everything and everyone else. It was an eye-opener: the world didn't stop when I did, everything carried on. Essay deadlines were postponed, my classes were taught by someone else, the kids were all fine. Fortunately, it wasn't a stroke but a rare form of migraine caused by stress – but I had learnt my lesson that I had to change, learn to relax more and stop burning the candle at both ends!'

Never lose the snooze

Along with spending time in nature, sleep is often the thing that is disregarded in our busy whirl of cramming stuff into our daily agendas – and the impact on the body and brain is serious and immediate. It is, after all, sleep that enables our bodies to rejuvenate and function properly during waking hours. NHS guidelines recommend that adults get around eight hours of sleep per night to function properly during the day. They say that losing one night's sleep will make you feel tired and irritable the next day, although it won't be damaging in the long term, but a persistent lack of sleep, where it is not valued and protected in your everyday life, can cause serious medical issues.

Our immune system is compromised without adequate rest, leaving us more susceptible to illness, and without the restful repair of our nervous systems we can experience slower reflexes and responses. Tiredness also puts our bodies on high alert, increasing the production of stress hormones and pushing up blood pressure, which in turn can lead to heart attacks and strokes. Sleep deprivation is also linked to inflammation, which increases the chances of heart disease, cancer and diabetes. A lack of quality shut-eye is known to lead to weight gain in people who routinely get fewer than seven hours per night due to, scientists believe, an increased level of ghrelin (the hunger-stimulating hormone) and a reduced level of leptin (the feeling-full hormone) being produced. Dull-looking skin and dreary eyes, which no amount of make-up will truly disguise, are visual downsides – and a lack of sleep makes our personality ugly, too. Tiredness makes us snappy, impatient and grumpy, with low levels of concentration. And a study of people getting fewer than six hours of sleep a night showed exaggerated levels of depression. All round, it is imperative that we revamp our schedules to prioritise sleep – good quality sleep!

Super slumber

Below are some little life edits to give yourself the best opportunity for sleep:

- Try to stick to a regular sleep pattern if you can, and get lots of bright sunlight during the day (leave the house!) and minimise bright lights at night. Don't watch television or work on a computer the half-hour before you want to sleep. Invest in blackout curtains.
- Cut caffeinated drinks and switch to something that soothes. A mug of golden milk (warm milk spiced with nutmeg, cinnamon, turmeric and ginger), lavender milk or Ovaltine will do the trick. Also cut down on heavy meals, alcohol and avoid drinking too much liquid in the hour before bedtime so that you're not on the loo all night.
- A bath before bed will bring on the zzzzzs. A drop in body temperature at night is one of the classic signals for the body to start producing melatonin, the hormone that induces sleep. Speed up the downward shift by heating yourself up artificially with a warm soak. Get out of a bath, cool yourself down for a while, then slip into bed. Keep your room cool (18°C is perfect). Adjust your bedding for the season.

- Listen to books or meditation apps, or close your eyes and try deep breathing, meditation and visualisation. Breathing in and out through your nostrils – in for four seconds, hold for four seconds, out for eight seconds – has a naturally sedating effect.
- Forget about what awaits you at work tomorrow, or panicking about getting enough sleep to be in tip-top condition. If worries or ideas are whirring, write them down so that you won't forget them, and relax knowing that they are safely stored.
- If you wake up in the middle of the night, don't toss and turn and feel irritated with yourself. Get up, cool yourself down and sit quietly, with soft light, and do something restful such as listening to calming music or reading a good book. Eat something small and light if your tummy is rumbling, take a sip of water but don't guzzle. Return to the comfort of your bed only when you feel yourself dozing off.

Own your story – here's how

It's time to check in and score and plan your most authentic life going forward. What health ticks can you add to your daily or weekly routine?

Accept limitations

Don't beat yourself up if you can't make time for an hour's gym session. Thirty, or even ten, minutes of movement is better than nothing.

*U*pgrade your habits

What traits should you ditch for a healthier life? What should you add? Simple, painless tweaks like snacking on nuts instead of chocolate, dumping cola for kombucha, or singing and stretching in the shower every morning will boost your body and your sense of self-control and self-esteem.

*T*reat yourself kindly

Reward a week of workouts with a massage or an Epsom salt soak. Reward yourself for a week of healthy eating with a fancy lunch or brunch with friends.

*H*elp yourself

If you're feeling lethargic or lumpy, join social groups – online or IRL – that engage in healthy behaviours and which can motivate you. They'll help you to revive your purpose.

*E*xpand your horizons

If your current workout routine is uninspiring, try something new, such as boxing, kayaking, a netball league. Find the fitness that keeps you invested.

*N*arrow down negative influences

You are allowed to refuse alcohol, so ignore peer pressure or comments about being boring. You're not at school any more. Often, negative comments are made because others know that you're doing a good thing that they wish they could! Also, avoid groups who are too focused ▶

on their external appearance over their internal beauty. They can get you obsessing over blown-up lips and Botox, when what really matters is how your heart looks.

Take time to improve your skills

Get better at adding mini health boosts into your life, such as taking the stairs, getting to bed 30 minutes earlier or cutting out caffeine after midday.

Improve your thinking

Are you coming from a place of wisdom and strength? Imagine yourself in a month, a year, ten years – how would you like to feel? Stronger, leaner, more supple?

Commit to your healthiest self

Wear sunscreen. Take multi-vitamins. Keep check-up appointments with your doctor and dentist. Your health is your most valuable commodity.

Chapter 4

Know Yourself, Show Yourself

'People become attached to their burdens sometimes more than the burdens are attached to them.'

George Bernard Shaw

So many of our problems come because we live in our heads. We can't escape the whirr, buzz, grind and flashes trapped in our skulls, or the demons and skeletons that refuse to slip out of our ears and let us rest quietly. If the heart is the warehouse of our emotions, the mind is the sorting office for our memories. Everything we've ever thought or felt is analysed, evaluated and filed. 'Memories are worse than bullets,' wrote Carlos Ruiz Zafon in one of my favourite gothic novels, *The Shadow of the Wind*. Truly, too often, it is mental exhaustion brought on by our past, more than current physical exhaustion, that reduces our ability to commit to a life we love; to give our all to the areas that deserve it. Instead of responding to a comment, dilemma or issue, we react to it, systematically dredging up past resentments, misdemeanours and injustices to tarnish current things that our life has thrown at us, disabling our ability to cope in a way that we would like.

To build a resilient cocoon within which we can healthily, happily reside, we have to appreciate our strengths, acknowledge our limitations and practise the self-kindness methods that work for us. A smart woman who has owned her purpose and ambition for decades in the face of so much public criticism and ridicule, Jennifer Lopez once said, 'sometimes you have to explore the darkness to get to the light and get back to who you are'. Be able to self-analyse. Be real. Be kind to yourself. Be comfortable in your own skin. The path to well-being starts with you, and the first few miles travelled take place within your head.

Get your head in the game

To own our lives authentically, we must first authentically own our thoughts – because it is those that make us what we are. Our height, weight, accent, facial features and wardrobe ... that's just decoration. As we walk through moods, moments and memories, we need to assemble the jumble into a manageable chunk. Here are some important things to remember:

- Your mind might be married to certain ways of doing things. We all have learnt behaviours and childhood imprinting to deal with. But, and it's a big but, we need to know that we can refocus, restart, readjust and revise how we think as often as we need to. Just knowing that you can edit your life is half the battle. You can do this alone with self-determination or with people who have

your back, or with a library full of inspiring and inform-
ative reads and a heart full of hope, or with a life coach
or a therapist who can guide you with practical advice.

- Hate is heavy and love is light. Reduce your mental
load by wishing people and propositions that have not
served you well good luck as you let them go – but do
let them go.

- Give your mind time to catch up with your heart; and
allow yourself to make mistakes or have relapses. As the
poet Yung Pueblo wrote 'sometimes you have to choose
health, life and love over and over again until your being
is ready to accept the new version of you'.

- It is always OK to express negative emotions, but try to
do so in a healthy way, otherwise you won't get healing,
you'll get guilt and regret. State your complaints when
you're calm, collected and have had time to see all the
angles. Only fools rush in. You have a voice, but it will
be more powerful if people have to concentrate while
they hear it.

- Don't overthink your goals or under-think your achievements. Allow yourself moments to reflect on what your
10-, 20-, 30-year-old self would think of what you've
achieved and how far you've gone. Don't always drag up
the failures, force yourself to regurgitate the successes,
too. I bet that if you saw yourself as your younger self
would, you'd remember you once dreamed of being
where, what or with whom you are now.

- Quieten your mind. The modern notion that you have to
be on the constant hunt, constant climb or in a constant
grind to be successful is rubbish. Rest, reflection and

allowing yourself to mentally recover from the assaults of the world are must-haves when building a happy life.

- Be careful whose voices you allow into your head. As Kyle Freedman stated eloquently, 'Don't take criticism from people you would never go to for advice.'

- Know your bandwidth. When your brain is feeling burnt out, go with it and hibernate. When your mind is feeling lonely, reach out and connect with people who love you.

- Feelings are not facts. When you feel unworthy, ugly, useless or just generally down, understand that this could be your hormones playing a trick on you – or your mind recalling insults you've been unfairly made to hear in the past. You might *feel* these things – but you are *not* these things. You are worthy, beautiful and effective.

- Remember, remember, remember the things that you *can* control (your thoughts, your words, your actions, your behaviour, your feelings) versus the things that you *cannot* control (others' thoughts, words, actions and feelings). Commit your head to thinking and being the best you can be and trusting your good intentions and ability to self-regulate.

Journal your journey – negative emotions

Sometimes we can feel like we're teetering on the edge of a cliff, the green grass of safety on one side while the murky depths of doom and gloom beckon us on the other; or that we're walking a tightrope and one minuscule flawed move will leave us flat on our face and unable to get up. There is too much noise, too many intrusions, too little time to decompress. If and when you feel like this, sit quietly and make a note of what has happened to throw you off balance, and why you think you are overwhelmed by such events. Next, follow this – my Self-Regulation Meditation:

1. Sit comfortably, somewhere peaceful and shut your eyes. Think back to the overwhelming emotions listed in your journal. Choose one.

2. Focus on each emotion at a time as you breathe in through your nose for four; picture the word for that emotion getting hot in your chest as you hold for four; now release it with a breath for eight, through your mouth, with an audible release if that feels good and natural to you.

3. Go through each overwhelming emotion in turn, repeating the breath pattern as many times as you need to.

4. When you've finished, open your eyes, and return to your journal. How do you feel now? Do you feel you've self-regulated your wild, overriding feelings? Do you feel that you've released them?

Don't become an actor in your own shit show

I had to give myself the shit-show pep talk recently, after a night out with friends went awry and I got myself wound up to the point of seeing a red mist, which soaked into my skin in a clammy layer of sadness that affected my mood for a whole week. It was silly really. It was at the festive meeting of my book club. We'd all agreed to meet at a friend's house in sequins and sparkles, and once we'd eaten all the cheese in the house, drunk all the wine (with hindsight, perhaps the flaw in our plan) and discussed the book, the option was on the table to turn the dial up on our monthly literary salon and head downtown to an eighties nightclub. It was Christmas, after all. Settled in, we picked up our books, did our customary thumbs up, middle or down – it had a mixed reaction across the group of eight – then I began reading the reader guide questions at the back.

We were all quite tipsy, and most of the group were so full of Stilton and Santa-shaped cookies by this point that they weren't very chatty and slipped back into the sofa cushions to listen, so a good friend and I took over. And we got carried away. We got pointed. We got emotional. We got accusatory. I'd shifted to sparkling water at this point, and wanted to jump off this speeding, scarily mean train heading to a full-on friend fight – but I wanted to prove my point! I wanted to defend my corner. My indignant inner teenager kept pushing on – half devil's advocate, half moral crusader – even when my chilled, low-conflict inner mama was shushing me to shut the fuck up.

If I'd engaged my brain, I'd have realised that I wasn't going to change her opinion, and she wasn't going to change mine. We should have gone dancing, but instead we'd climbed a steep hill, and we were both determined to die on it. I was homesick (we couldn't go back to England for Christmas and I missed my family with a visceral ache) and hormonal (my period was due the next day); we'd both drunk too much. All this meant I wasn't in charge of my emotions sufficiently enough to check my motives. Was I trying to show off? Was I trying to be clever? Was I trying to wind her up? All were unsavoury reasons to continue bickering when we could have been shimmering under a mirror ball to A-ha's 'Take on Me'. Eventually, we got ourselves into an Uber. I couldn't sleep that night and woke up to texts from two friends asking if I was OK. I wasn't. I felt foolish and sad, and I imagined my sparring partner – who is sweet and as sensitive as me – would be feeling bad about her part in it, too, which made me feel even worse.

I made an important life edit in the aftermath of that experience; one that has served me well since and helped me to gain a mental calmness: I don't have to share my opinion about everything. I don't have to fall on my sword to defend every single thought I ever have. I can choose my battles and hold my peace when I haven't got the mental strength for a fight, or the stomach for a mental onslaught. I should continue to read and research, ask people for their stories and statistics, and trust my gut – but not feel the need to push my knowledge on other people, especially when I'm feeling vulnerable or uncomfortable.

One friend I told this story to, and shared the news of my subsequent change, told me that I should be stronger. 'You have a right to a voice,' she said. 'Just learn to stay away from people who think you're arguing with them every time you try to express yourself. You should be able to debate issues that matter in a safe space without feeling personally attacked.' Ten years ago, I would have agreed with her; and I still do in areas where my voice has impact and I've weighed up the pros and cons of sticking my head above the parapet, prepared to take a few verbal blows for a better reason than my inflamed ego. But in other times, when I'm feeling introverted, exhausted or delicate, I can calmly and authentically go the way of Rumi: yesterday I was clever, so I wanted to change the world. Today I am wise, so I am changing myself. I can live with unexpressed thoughts if it safeguards my mental well-being.

The news of the world

Sometimes simply checking your social media, picking up a newspaper or turning on the television can feel like a physical and mental affront. Is anything decent and pleasant happening out there? You wouldn't know because we are bombarded with bad, sad and mad information, with little indication that there is anything positive in the world. Of course, we need to stay informed and educated, but we need to protect our minds from overstressing about things we cannot change, too. An essay in the *British Journal of Psychology* entitled 'The psychological impact of negative TV news bulletins: The catastrophising of personal worries' investigated how watching negative material exacerbated an anxious and sad mood in participants of the study, and it also increased their tendency to 'catastrophise a personal worry'. When it comes to your mental well-being you can say, 'Stop the world, I want to get off!' Here's how:

Concentrate on being the change you want to see You cannot solve climate change or racial inequality on your own, for example, but you can control what you and your household consume, you can keep yourself up to date with the latest scientific research and you can look at how your behaviours positively or negatively affect outcomes. Go micro when macro is too much. Use your power where it can help: in your family, your school and your community. A change at ground roots level will help you feel better. Donate to a good cause, volunteer your time to a local charity, reach out to your support network and see how you can come together to make a difference. Learn to listen without placing yourself at the centre of a cause, write to your government ministers asking for change, read books and essays or watch documentaries or movies that allow you to question your assumptions.

Seek out the good news Unfollow people who wind you up on Facebook and Instagram, turn off Twitter, and search out the good vibes and good souls. Fill your feeds with uplifting quotes, spiriting news about reaching goals from organisations you value, and allow yourself to drift into comedy-clip territory on YouTube. In trying times, I dig out beloved bubblegum on Netflix. Nights in with a *Frasier, The West Wing* or *The Durrells* marathon is mentally restorative.

Focus on being present If we allow ourselves to worry about things buried in the past, or way off into the future, we'll feel our control slipping away as we slip down dark, dreary rabbit holes. Stay in the moment. And remember that worrying about things outside our immediate capabilities or jurisdiction is as useful as a chocolate teapot.

Allow yourself to cover your ears and eyes when you know you can't take it. During depressing election cycles, I switch off the news before bed and just get the headlines each morning. This helps me to sleep better. There's so much noise in our 24/7 news climate, but we don't have to hear it all.

Accept uncertainty: the world has always had tough times, violent times and sad times, we just know more about it now because everyone is screaming at us. Instead of living for minute-by-minute drama, however addictive it can be, remove yourself, and steady yourself with rituals that help your head.

As humans we are conditioned to have a negative bias: we remember the one rude comment more clearly than the ten positive ones, and we remember the one horrid news story more than the ten wonderful things that we've witnessed humans do today. Be aware of this bias, and let it inform what and how you consume information.

Give yourself permission to let things slip

Sometimes we turn down invitations because we have other plans, we have to work, or we need a night on the sofa in our pyjamas. Sometimes, an invite can trigger something that we don't feel strong enough to cope with, and we have to be kind to ourselves and acknowledge that. Perhaps one of the fellow guests is an ex-partner you're not over, or perhaps the group of friends gathering makes you feel anxious about your current place in the world. Own those feelings, and say no. I've had this twice in my life. The first time was when I was a freshly minted divorcée, aged 30, and everyone else around me seemed to be falling hopelessly in love and getting hitched. As the first of my friends to get divorced, I was a walking, talking antithesis to the 'happy ever after' dream, and found sitting in a wedding congregation as a vicar talked about 'til death do us part' very difficult. I felt like a fraud in all things love; a black lump of realism among the pastel shades of romantic optimism.

At first, I'd accept the invites out of a sense of duty, travel however many miles, a gift under my arm, to watch other people coo and tease and hope to catch the bouquet on the dance floor at the end of the night. Usually, I'd end up drunk at the bar, with a few random fellow cynics, feeling lesser and counterfeit, humiliated by my own failure to make my first marriage work. After a year of this, I started rejecting wedding invitations, sending gifts and well-wishes, and started working on getting my heart back to a place where I could genuinely be happy for other people's happiness.

The second time I stopped saying yes to invitations was when I was struggling to stay pregnant. Over a period of three years I suffered three miscarriages, and the sight of a baby bump or a tot in a pram could have me rushing away and crumpling into a heap in the nearest available place to hide. As you can imagine, the idea of attending a baby shower or a gender-reveal party – where everything is pregnancy and baby-focused (the decorations, the games, the food) – was just too heartbreaking to deal with. My husband didn't understand and found my inability to attend these celebrations embarrassing, but I had to be honest with myself. I was a mess, every pregnancy announcement felt like a dagger through my womb, and I just couldn't do it. Again, I sent gifts and well-wishes, but I allowed myself to give credence to my emotions, and say no. You can do this, too. If you want to explain why, you can. If you don't feel up to it, you don't have to. Look after your fragile heart and mental health in all things.

Getting real: Claire, 41

'I was fortunate to learn the satisfaction of a good physical and mental declutter long before Marie Kondo came along. I embraced it wholeheartedly once I had children and the detritus of plastic paraphernalia and irrational worry that accompanies little people threatened to spill out of its allocated storage space – and my mind. Now I use a good decluttering session as therapy: there's nothing more satisfying than carrying bin bags full of outgrown clothes and toys to the charity shop, cancelling events I don't want to attend, and saying no to random requests the children make if I know we can't squeeze them in fruitfully. After a good house edit, I survey the results of my work with pride and a certain smugness. I will even confess to taking before-and-after selfies and then sending them to a friend I know will admire my handiwork and give me the praise my children wouldn't! The sense of peace this gives my overactive mind is undeniable, and I am a huge believer in the beneficial crossover to all aspects of your life of a neat, edited environment.'

Overthinking: a crime story

A clever and anonymous philosopher has bestowed me with my favourite quote on the self-inflicted injury of overthinking. 'When you're 20, you care what everyone thinks, when you're 40, you stop caring what everyone thinks, when you're 60, you realise no one was thinking about you in the first place.' We do push ourselves, don't we? Unnecessarily so! Our brains are for ever switched on and make up completely ridiculous scenarios in our heads much of the time. Instead of trusting our gut and going for something, we second-guess ourselves – or third- or fourth-guess ourselves – which is not only a waste of our time, but can also be bad for our mental health. Stop overthinking, start living and ...

- Let go of a fear of failure. So what if you make a mistake? You'll build resilience, diplomacy and quick-thinking skills. Mistakes give you the chance to share and grow.
- Shush the negative self-talk and silence the self-doubt. You can make decisions that are right for you. You are the best person to know what you need.
- Practice. When a dilemma arises, note your first reaction. Now muse on it for an hour, overthink to your little heart's content. Make a decision. Now return to your notes. Are they eerily similar? Go through this practice enough until you've honed your thought processes and you trust yourself more. It will save you time in the long run.
- Be aware that overthinking might be a symptom of

something else: do you need to address a wider issue such as anxiety or depression? Do you need to get a certain naysayer or negativity purveyor out of your ear-hole – and headspace?

- Put things into perspective. Catch yourself next time you drift off into an overly panicked state of worry or confusion. Is the worst-case scenario likely? Could you actually benefit from just going with a decision?
- Give yourself a time frame. If you know that you like to judge and value every single idea, set a timer. Don't allow things to drag out and seep into other areas of your life. Make your overthinking a part of your daily routine. Allow yourself a half-hour every morning to chew over your niggles, make decisions and move on. Don't do this at night if it stops you from getting a good night's rest.
- Abandon the idea of perfection. You'll be overthinking and under-doing for ever if you wait for it. Go with the good-for-now and good-enough method of making decisions, rather than the set-in-stone-for-eternity-so-it-had-better-be-100-per-cent-perfect method (certain major life changes excluded, naturally). You can't predict the future, so why try? Just accept the best on offer, and make it work for you.

Oversharing: a slime story

Our culture has us believe that we should never have an undisclosed thought or unexposed midriff. We are told that sharing is caring, unloading is emboldening and that we must constantly join the chatter. I mean, if you weren't captured while having a deep and meaningful conversation with a friend on Instagram, did it even really happen? I am essentially an open book – er, really? – but I have a few rules. I only overshare *my* shame, no one else's. I tell *my* story, but it's up to other people to tell their own – if they want to. And I don't implicate people in my social-media crimes: I might look decent in a photo, but if a friend is squinting, it's not going to be uploaded.

I have a code: we all look and sound good, or none of us look or sound good. For the same reason, I don't overshare things that my children will find embarrassing in their futures either. Run everything through a filter first: will anyone take offence or be upset? Take a good-taste edit. Other good ideas to think about when wanting to divulge include:

- Why do you want attention for this particular thing? Do you think it could help someone, or are you so happy that you want to spread the glee? Or are you adding it to your social-media memory maker to look back on for ever? Do you need moral support from those you love? Are you taking ownership of your story? These are all good reasons. If you're oversharing because you're looking for sympathy with the wrong crowd, or you're looking to get attention from a certain someone you don't have a more meaningful relationship with, or you're showing off to boost your wilted ego, na-ha! These are not reasons to share anything – in person or online.
- You might get reactions that make a situation worse. It's best to sit with your dilemma for a bit, whether

negative or positive, then go to trusted friends or a professional such as a teacher or therapist if you do not want external input.

- Remember that once something is out there, it's out there for ever. Yes, future employers can see you whining about your ex-boyfriend or see the cute photo you shared of your hungover-but-still-hot-after-a-full-on-night-out ass. If you wouldn't want your next boss, your mum or your first teacher to see it or hear it, don't share it.

- We are told that oversharing makes us authentic and brave, but sometimes it makes us look vain, glib or daft. Focus more on the one-to-one moments you share with people, and work on the interior you, before you try to build up the exterior persona you want to share. Ignore the few examples you hear about oversharing getting someone fame and fortune. Normally regret is more forthcoming.

Decompression sessions

We're always getting knocked, bothered and manipulated, aren't we? Our worries, insecurities and fears follow us into our bedroom at night, eyeing us up from a screen, the last thing we see as we try to sleep at night. Bad news beckons 24/7. The inescapable feelings of doom and gloom are there at the push of a button, shouting at us to get anxious about the future or die. And all this is what we choose to partake in. We have all this anxiety on top of all the very real things we have to be concerned about: the welfare of our loved ones, our jobs, our bank accounts, running a home, our own physical and mental health. We can switch off from some of it, sometimes, but lots of it we have no choice about. We need methods of reducing the mental burnout we feel, and re-establishing balance and calm when we can. Luckily, there are many free, easy and scientifically proven great ways to get our minds back into a healthy place – and that is what matters.

Meditation

Taking time to meditate isn't a luxury. It will save you time from worry and feeling run-down in the long run – and it really is as simple as being still, closing your eyes and clearing your mind. Meditation is just a special word for musing, reflecting and contemplation. There are many apps and YouTube videos available to help you get started – and you should start. Scientists from the University of California and Harvard Medical School got together to compare the benefits of taking a holiday and doing regular meditation and were astounded by the results. They used 64 female novice meditators between the ages of 30 and 60, and 30 experienced meditators from the same demographic. The women were sent to the same resort, half taking part in a meditation programme, the other half not. Surveys and blood samples were taken from the women at the start and end of the six days of the study period, and after ten months. The women who meditated showed fewer symptoms of depression and anxiety than the ones who hadn't, with their blood work showing significant and positive genetic changes related to immune function and stress response.

Make the edit Start simply. Find a quiet, peaceful spot in your home, garden or anywhere you feel safe, sit cross-legged or lie down if more comfortable, and close your eyes. Practise taking full, deep, rhythmic breaths. Breathe in for eight, hold for four, breathe out for eight. Repeat as often as feels good. Add words to the sound of your inhalation and exhalation if you want to. A favourite of mine is to repeat in my head 'I inhale the future' as I'm breathing in, 'I exhale the past', as I'm breathing out. It keeps me focused on my breath and the choice I am making to edit my way to a life I love, forgiving myself past mistakes.

Scriptotherapy

There have been times in my life when writing has worked as therapy for me. The best example I can share was when I lost a longed-for pregnancy, 14 weeks along. Grief-stricken, I turned to words for solidarity, support and self-expression. When I couldn't articulate my despair to my family, and I sat mute to the concerns of my husband and parents, pen and paper became my only tools of survival. I would sit at home, trapped in my head and write countless poems, to release the pain, then edit them ruthlessly, or read them over and over again, pages of my diary falling apart, dampened by tears and covered in a desperate scrawl.

This self-revelation was powerful, each sentence allowing me to process and clarify my feelings around my loss of identity and motherhood. It didn't have to be good, I didn't have to share it, but I could read Virginia Woolf, Sylvia Plath and Doris Lessing, take inspiration from them and make my own story.

At the time, I was in the middle of an MA in literature and taking a class on trauma narrative with Dr Suzette A. Henke. When I told her one day after class why I was withdrawn, and how I had been compiling trauma narratives of my own to try to cope with my mental anguish, she sympathised, then congratulated me for having such a healthy response. An expert in her field, years earlier she had coined the term for this process I and countless other people had gone through, Scriptotherapy. Dr Henke explained to me how we'd been using words to heal for centuries – in letters to faraway sisters, in diary entries, in declarations to evil stepmothers – that no one would ever read.

Far from being a vain, self-centred approach to healing and mental well-being, as I had feared, Scriptotherapy is undergoing something of a resurgence, and is popular within modern psychology thanks to its ability to offer healing without confrontation, to give closure without reproach. Writing can unleash the subconscious even more than Freud's 'talking cure'. Nothing is repressed because we feel we have control over the ink and paper. As Dr Henke states in the introduction to her book on the topic *Shattered Subjects*:

> The authorial effort to reconstruct a story of psychological debilitation could offer potential for mental healing and begin to alleviate persistent symptoms of numbing, dysphoria and uncontrollable flashbacks. Autobiography could so effectively mimic the scene of psychoanalysis that life-writing might provide a therapeutic alternative for victims of severe anxiety and, more seriously, of post-traumatic stress disorder.

I improved with every swoosh of my pen: my emotional trauma sucked onto the page and out of my heart. My Scriptotherapy eventually became my master's thesis and I graduated four days before giving birth to a healthy son, named after William Blake – the English poet who had kept me going up to campus to study when I didn't think I could get out of bed. And thanks to the notes I kept during that dark time, I can handle the tough times of raising a child, because I can read how I felt when I thought that being a mother would never be a part of my story.

Make the edit Journaling is a great place to start. Find yourself a notebook that makes you happy, a pen you love to write with, and set yourself a place in which to sit. Make daily lists of things that make you happy, things you could improve and things you'd like to try tomorrow. If you haven't got the will to start writing, read more. Find authors who boost your mood and teach you important lessons.

Art therapy

Like journaling, using art as a way of self-expression is a great route to working through your thoughts and emotions. Creativity allows you to intuit, feel and understand yourself and to remove the roadblocks to self-improvement. To take a sketch-pad or easel to a peaceful spot in the wilderness to draw or paint your pain using the landscape and your imagination is remedial. Venting on paper – with a pen, pencil or paintbrush – is a safe haven, a private place, where you can truly be yourself and begin to heal with honesty. And no one has to see what you've done if you don't want them too, so you are wonderfully free to reveal your most authentic self.

Make the edit Join a local art class if you are attached to the community aspect of it, or get yourself some supplies and follow online art instruction. YouTube has excellent draw-along videos. If you don't fancy art, try crafts: knitting, crocheting, flower arranging, woodworking. They are all great distractions. And if you don't want to do it yourself, take trips to local art galleries and exhibitions and give yourself time to just be still, and gawp in awe and wonder.

Forest bathing

Walking in a forest feels good and smells good, and we know we should be doing it, but in our busy schedules – packed with meetings, gym trips, bar hopping and staring blank-faced at devices – finding the time to engage with nature is often the first thing we cut back on. This is a shame. Spending time outside, in fresh air, soaking up vitamin D and observing the world around us, offers universal, countless and free well-being benefits. Reconnecting with nature reduces stress.

We're saying yes too often, taking on too much, then thinking about everything too deeply, which makes us obsessively worried about the 'mental overload' of modern living. Meanwhile, the cure to reduce it is literally on our doorstep. While I was researching a previous book, *Forest Therapy: Seasonal Ways to Embrace Nature for a Happier You!*, I was overwhelmed by the facts and figures highlighting how connecting with nature was an invaluable source of mental and physical well-being.

For example, research published in the *Journal of Environmental Psychology* shows that being exposed to restorative environments, such as a forest, lake or beach, restores mental energy, and that natural beauty inspires feelings of awe which gives a secondary brain boost. Spending time looking at plants, birds, or any of the small details in the magical living world, allows our brain to switch off and change gear, which allows it to step up and focus better with improved patience when we return to work or study.

Environmental psychologists at the University of Michigan investigated how the visual elements of nature – looking at a stream, a sunrise, a butterfly or an ancient tree – affected a person's mental fatigue. They discovered that looking at these soft, natural wonders allowed the brain to recuperate, recover and rest after coping with the constant man-made assaults of modern living, then give it a fresh approach to problems. The brain in nature is more open to reflect, daydream and wander, which boosts creativity. The psychologists noted that the benefits of spending time in nature even lasted for a while after heading back indoors, so a stroll in a park before an important brainstorming meeting could be something to think about.

A brisk march in the fresh air will make you feel happier, too. A study in *Environmental Science and Technology* found a link between decreased anxiety and bad moods with walks in the woods, while another reported that taking a walk outdoors should be prescribed by doctors as a supplement to existing treatments for depressive disorders. The *Journal of Affective Disorders* released an analysis that declared how every green, natural environment (not just forests) improved self-esteem, a crucial element for personal happiness, and that the presence of water – a lake, a river, the ocean – made the positive effects on happiness even more noticeable. A study by the University of Essex backed up these findings, revealing how just five minutes of physicality in a green space lifted spirits and self-confidence in participants.

Make the edit There are little tweaks that you can start doing immediately, even if you haven't got an hour spare to go for a nature walk (although, by the way, you have – just put your phone down). Small things like waking up and not immediately checking your weather app to see what you should wear that day but actually looking out the window, checking the movement of the clouds, how the wind is pushing through the trees, or listening out for birds beckoning in the morning with a gleeful chorus. At night, don't go straight for the glare of a television screen or YouTube page. Take a moment to look outside, notice the sky changing colour, the visibility of the stars, the sounds of night. It never hurt anyone to disengage from their day with a quiet minute, breathing in the cool night air, calmly preparing for bedtime away from the barrage of entertainment and the junk light that crowds our lives.

Mini distractions

When you need to switch off but you only have five minutes:

- Go out into your garden, smell the flowers and take five deep breaths.

- Practise visualisation techniques: build an image of what is negative in your mind, then watch it shrinking or drowning. Now imagine a positive outcome, and make it glow and enlarge.
- Dance to your favourite pop song (turned up loud).
- Paint your nails, apply a face-mask, or jump in the shower while listening to a podcast.
- Drift off in a daydream. Allow your mind to float to new places.
- Give someone you love a hug.
- Phone a friend.
- Drink a glass of cold water.
- Read a short story or poem.

Can hardship help?

We are always searching for new ways to keep our calm, limit stress and stay happy. Compared to our ancestors, we have never been richer, healthier or lived longer, but despite all this, maintaining good mental health is a constant struggle, especially when sudden changes, bad news or global disasters knock us to the floor. Sometimes these struggles are invaluable to us, though, allowing us to re-evaluate what is important. With this theory in mind, there has been a recent movement that recommends a self-flagellation of sorts, a removal of excess and the reduction of everyday luxury in the belief that when it is returned to us we will experience an elevated sense of gratitude and appreciation for the small, simple things in life. Our universal suffering through the Covid-19 pandemic provided this opportunity on an unprecedented scale; a once in a lifetime lockdown that forced us to consider our gratitude for what we once took for granted, and an acknowledgement of what we would appreciate more when 'normal' life resumed.

A recent essay by the Harvard Medical School tells us how feeling gratitude makes us happier, because it reminds us to acknowledge the goodness in our life rather than filling our head with the negatives, while reminding us that we are not owed anything. We look at each element in our life with a renewed joy that we'd previously taken for granted. Advocates insist that when we know how it feels to be hungry, ill, scared or confused, we will never take our creature comforts for granted again, and our empathy will be raised. Indeed, as my friends, family and I worried about those among us who had caught the coronavirus, or lost jobs because of it, or felt like failures as they attempted to home-school their children when the schools were shut down, there was a resounding and magnificent appreciation for what we still had – we could still sing, dance, read, talk to loved ones, watch films, try new hobbies, go for a walk or a bike ride and hear the birds singing or see the flowers blooming. Very quickly into the lockdown I also noticed a communal hope that we would all come together and recognise lessons to be learnt and changes that we would carry forward. 'When the dust settles,' a friend emailed three months into the coronavirus lockdown, 'we will realise how little we really need, how very much we have, and the true value of human connection and small, simple liberties.'

Journal your journey – gratitude

Being thankful and expressing it – through scribbling down thoughts in a gratitude journal, telling loved ones how they make you feel, reflecting on your good luck at the end of each day – can give us a mental and physical boost. And this practice can also remind us that happiness and healing do not come from material goods but from restorative habits and simple pleasures like a long soak in a bath after a hard day, or that first sip of tea in the morning, or observing a particularly clear and starry sky at night. Start noting down things that bring you joy when you notice them, and look back at them when you feel down.

Getting real: Sunny, 41

'I once heard that those who live in the past, experience depression and those who live in the future, experience anxiety, so I have been working on staying in the moment, and learning to say no to things I know won't serve my mental health. My mum has terrible boundaries and often agrees to things, or worse she offers her help and time and then gets irritated about it, as if it is someone else's fault. This is all unintentional, but it did make me want to evaluate my boundaries before I became the same way. If I can attend an event, I am there because I truly want to be. If I don't get excited by the invitation, I decline straight away, because I do not want to be known as a flake. When I host a function, I genuinely only want people there who want to be and this is why I am comfortable saying no and I hope for the same courtesy in return.'

The glory in gratitude

A study published in *Emotion*, a psychology journal, proved how acknowledging people's contribution to your world, by thanking them in person, or by note, or just by your behaviour towards them, will make you more likeable and popular, thereby improving your social life. Mentally, an attitude of gratitude reduces the amount of time we get weighed down and worried by toxic emotions. Research in the *Journal of Environmental Psychology* explained how experiencing feelings of awe and gratitude while spending time in nature led to increased positivity and creativity. When we're feeling grateful, we feel uplifted and our self-esteem is less battered by what other people are achieving or receiving around us. Studies have also found that when we feel grateful for our lives, we take better care of our physical health, exercising regularly and going for regular check-ups, and a study in *Applied Psychology: Health and Wellbeing* journal revealed that writing down a few positive sentiments before going to bed helped people to sleep deeper and longer as well – another massive health benefit.

I learnt the power of gratitude as a mental-health tool after I moved to New York City in 2005, an exciting but scary time for me: alone, with an intimidating job to do and all the pressure that came with it. For the first six months I'd encountered a level of emotional outbursts and oversharing from my American colleagues that was foreign to me and made me feel a bit uncomfortable. As Thanksgiving approached, I imagined more of the same: cheesy declarations of gratitude. What I didn't expect was the seriousness with which my new American friends held the beautiful question at the heart of the holiday: what are you thankful for? My first Thanksgiving dinner was eaten with a hodgepodge group of displaced Americans, adventurous Argentinians and British colleagues. As we sat at the table in front of the gluttonous feast, the Americans led us in a sharing circle. I raised an eyebrow at a fellow Londoner across the table and she smirked back.

Then they began: sharing the gratitude they felt for a brother's sobriety, a mother's negative test result, a pay rise that allowed them to finally move into an apartment with air conditioning. I felt mean and childish. To be open and vulnerable is something we often ridicule Americans for, but I was moved. When it was finally my turn to speak, I expressed how thankful I was to have met such a warm group of people in this huge, strange city, and I thanked the host for welcoming me into her home, allowing me to spend this time with new friends – and I meant every word from the bottom of my cold, English heart. Sceptical me got teary then, and has done at every Thanksgiving since, whether in a group or on my own, as I've taken the time to muse on what I have to be grateful for, something that we rarely take the time to do unless prompted, and it's a habit that I have brought into my daily life.

Own your story – here's how

It's time to check in and get to know your own mind. Note down what does and doesn't serve your mental health, and plan how to live your most authentic, happy life going forward.

Accept that you have mental limitations

Sometimes it won't serve you to take on too much. Only do something that is necessary or brings joy; you don't have to be all things at all times.

Understand your anxieties

Work out what is keeping you awake at night and why? What can be deleted or rewritten? Can you prescribe yourself some time out?

Tread lightly when times are tough

If you're feeling low and your mind is overworking, go into self-preservation mode: hibernate, say no, switch off or switch over. Fill your day with tiny treats: fresh flowers by your bed, a blast of pop on the radio during your commute, wearing your favourite dress, re-reading sweet emails or letters from old friends.

Happy starts in the head

Without peace of mind, we can't find peace anywhere else, so value your boundaries and try not to step over them. Close your eyes and imagine yourself drawing a circle around yourself – your precious, special,

▶

darling self – and picture it whenever you are confronted with a challenge. Should you let this event or person encroach on your circle?

*E*njoy alone time
Silence allows an overworked brain to rejuvenate itself. There is a difference between being alone and loneliness.

*N*arrow down your mental clutter collection
Chuck out old, bad ideas and streamline your thoughts to ones that work. Just because something has traditionally been done a certain way, it doesn't mean that it's the right way.

*T*ake time to forgive
Say 'thanks for that experience, I've grown because of it' and move on.

*I*nstall a mental 'archive'
where you can send unhelpful info.

*C*hange your negative brain waves with a few deep breaths
Ten minutes of 8–4–8 can help: breathe in for eight, hold for four, and breathe out for eight. Give yourself a literal breather.

Chapter 5

A Change Would Do You Good

'They always say time changes things,
but you actually have to change them yourself.'

Andy Warhol

Test your mettle. If something isn't giving you what you need, change it. Yes, it might take courage, it might cause upset, it might lead to accusations of rocking the boat or getting too big for your boots, or of putting yourself first (how dare you!), but remember: you only get one go at this glorious, scary, wonderful life. If you need to edit it frequently, judiciously and courageously to give yourself the best chance of health and happiness, you must do it.

Our bodies and brains are programmed to do the same thing over and over, and routine and ritual are positive things when continued cycles are beneficial to your mental and physical well-being. But when you're feeling stuck in a dead end or unfulfilled, a change in any part of your life can be intellectually stimulating (where opinions and assumptions are challenged), mentally rewarding (moving cities, travelling to new places and meeting different people broaden your horizons) and allows real personal growth (change teaches you flexibility, adaptability and openness). You get to find out who you really are when you're in the flux of change – what you're really made of – and you get to have fun, because a change really can be as good as a rest.

Taylor Swift is someone who's changed before our eyes; we've watched her go from 13 to 30 years old under a spotlight, a test case in the laboratory of public opinion. In her 2020 documentary, *Miss Americana*, she says that she was told from the very start of her career to hide her personality, shy away from her authenticity to fit in, to sell. 'Nice girls don't force their opinion on people. A nice girl smiles and waves and says thank you. I became the person everyone wanted me to be.' But pleasing everyone else and hiding her true self made her anxious and rather sad. What did she do as she approached her thirtieth birthday looking for an authentic, happier life? She took a year off and performed one of the biggest public life edits we've seen in Celebville. 'I had to deconstruct an entire belief system. Toss it out and reject it. It woke me up from constantly feeling like I was fighting for people's respect. It was happiness without anyone else's input.' She stopped saying yes to the men in suits, cut back on the fake friendships, threw the muzzle off and started living a life that she loved.

We all have a bit of Taylor in us. If we're feeling misunderstood, unrepresented, bullied, silenced, picked apart – as she was, as we've all felt at various times in our lives – we need to look at what we can do to mend our sad hearts and anxious brains. We can shake it off. We can't wait around for the world to catch up with us and see us on our level – we have to take control.

Be your own force for change

Before making any big decisions or doing any major life edits, take stock of what you want to lose and what you want to gain.

Do you need to make changes? If you've been feeling lacklustre, frustrated or unhappy for a while now, you do need to change something. And it is down to you. Continuing to blame other people for your predicament will only get you so far. Yes, people – even friends and family who you know love you – can be a drain and a pain, but real meaningful change needs to come from within. Because that is the only change you have 100 per cent control over. And you'll get such a boost in self-worth when you achieve what you need to.

Are you feeling strong? Because putting a new you out there takes courage, and you might face resistance from corners you never even considered. Wait until you are ready, trust that your heart and head are tight and right on this development, and be prepared for kickback. People love to gossip, gloat and say they told you so. You are perfectly entitled to do a Kate Moss: never complain, never explain. Refuse to engage in judgements around your progressive decision to make meaningful changes.

Change is inevitable as we age and the world marches on around us. As George Bernard Shaw wrote, 'Progress is impossible without change.' Resistance to it can be futile and cause us to get left behind, but don't feel the need to throw everything out. Embrace the future with curiosity and enthusiasm while securely holding on to your morals, values and the people you adore. Don't change for change's sake.

When considering how you can change, focus on being yourself, not on being popular. You cannot chase cool. You can only chase the most authentic version of you, which also happens to be the coolest.

Nourish yourself What could you feed your soul to be happier and healthier? Change your life to make it a more fruitful buffet of things that satisfy your appetite, not what your peers tell you to eat, or society tells you to snack on. Write up your own menu.

Feeling nervous about making a change? Write yourself a letter, or look at yourself in the mirror and talk firmly. Explain on the page or out loud to your reflection why you're making these adaptations, what you hope for and how you'll achieve your goals.

Don't ever make rash decisions about huge changes in a flash of boredom. Sit with decisions for a while, wrestle with them through different moods, moments and hormone spikes. A flicker of boredom is not a reason to dismantle a relationship, a career or a home; a sustained period of consideration is.

As you make healthy changes in your life, you'll become a lighthouse for those around you who hope to make similar adjustments in their lives. A few people might not congratulate you (envy, anger or unhappiness could be to blame for that), but people who really admire you will ask for advice, bask in your success and feel proud of you. You'll become an inspiration, a sensation, a symbol of what is possible. Always share your tips, but never crow.

Do muster your courage and make the change you need. Do step up. As Trevor Noah eloquently explains, 'I'm consumed with regret for the things I didn't do, the choices I didn't make, the things I didn't say ... regret is the thing we should fear most. Failure is an answer. Rejection is an answer. Regret is an eternal question you will never have the answer to.' Be the change, make the move. No regrets.

Major milestones and making the change

Some life edits will take the book that is you in a whole new direction. Some twists and turns are fabulous and written by their author, other plot points are thrown at your plans and can be hard to navigate. But you must navigate them! My yoga teacher says, 'what you ingest, make sure you digest'. Everything you take in goes through you and comes out again: people, experiences, changes. Think carefully about the big things that will stay in your system for a while. You are allowed to sweat the big stuff, but give yourself the best chance of surviving it.

- Make time for yourself while making big decisions. Your brain needs time to mull over scenarios away from external influences and expectations. You need time to sit with your own thoughts, ambitions and goals. Daydream about your future. What do you deserve?
- Know your options, and know they are ever-evolving.

Assess the pros and cons, and the financial and mental costs, get yourself a mentor or a close-knit group of people who have walked the path before you and are prepared to go back and walk a bit of it again with you to share what they learnt.

- Don't beat yourself up. Rather than being self-critical, be self-aware. You're going through some things – it's a challenge. Treat yourself the way you would treat a friend: with kindness. Getting angry with yourself for falling behind schedule or not executing something perfectly won't help anyone, least of all you.
- Build your stamina. Know what you need to keep going in a new direction. Does music motivate you? Do you find that alone time replenishes you? Or do you need to change your daily sleeping and eating habits to get you through these new changes? Give yourself the tools you need.
- Focus on one change at a time. Give yourself the time to succinctly define what you want to achieve, how long you want to give yourself to achieve it, and how you are going to get there. The enthusiasm or despair that has inspired this desire for change should be tempered with an achievable outline.

Making a move

Leaving your family home or home town can feel equally terrifying and exciting. As bright, shiny new landscapes open up, the nourishing familiarity of what you have always known and loved is gone, and life can feel pretty bittersweet. Whether you're going off to university, or leaving your parents' house to move around the corner, or you're flying across an ocean and saying au revoir to your homeland, these changes need to be noted and your feelings respected. Prepare yourself for a move by being organised and making preparations in good time, to keep anxiety away. Focus on the positive reasons why you are moving (the chance to learn, a fabulous new job, a loving relationship) rather than the negatives. The world is a small place now thanks to technology, so even if your move is a long-distance one, you will still be able to keep up with friends and family. Allow yourself to say proper goodbyes, not just to people, but also to places you love and routines you've had for a while. And plan in advance things to keep you going once you've landed in your new country or city: join relevant groups on social media, buy membership to a theatre or museum, volunteer, and when you get there, find the coffee shop you want to make your own, the park you plan to walk in, and start building new rituals.

When I left London to move to New York when I was 29 years old, I felt invigorated and alive, full of possibility. Frank Sinatra's promise that if I made it there, I'd make it anywhere serenaded my skull, putting a skip in my step, as I made my way along Fifth Avenue from my apartment to my office every morning. But in quiet moments, struggling to sleep, or unsure which of my new friends really understood me, my homesickness was unbearable. I spent a lot of my first year as an expat dashing between the two countries I now called home, and my Manhattan apartment was plastered with photos of my loved ones, my sofa covered in Union Jack cushions, my cupboard full of Marmite and HP sauce. Homesickness and nostalgia are hard things to battle through, but I coped by knowing that I could always go back, and then realising that when I did return home nothing had really changed. I'd grown, explored, had gained insight into a whole new culture … and I went home and sat in the same pub with the same people sharing the same love and affection. I still belonged. I just belonged to two places now.

A fellow immigrant to America recently shared this on her Instagram page, and it sums up perfectly the pleasure and pain in changing countries – even changing cities: *you will never be completely at home again, because part of your heart will always be elsewhere. That is the price you pay for the richness of loving and knowing people in more than one place.*

An array of tiny moments can make me miss people – or subtle cultural nuances – with a staggering sadness. When I'm feeling low, or misunderstood, I often rose-tint my way back to my London friends, my Essex family home, my university days in Canterbury, and I get teary with longing for them. But as academic Svetlana Boym sensibly noted: 'The imperative of a contemporary nostalgia is to be homesick and sick of home – occasionally at the same time.' So, I honour my feelings around my geographic change (eat baked beans on hot buttered toast, listen to BBC podcasts or watch Bridget Jones movies), while appreciating all the mind-expanding opportunities that being able to merge in with a new city, country and culture has given me.

Office politics

Leaving a job you dislike or that no longer serves you is a necessary but often hard life edit to make. When you know that you're climbing the wrong ladder, or you're following the wrong path, or you've run out of places to go, you have to change direction – but how? It's all about getting the right mix. You need to be true to your long-term aims and goals while considering your current economic needs. Can you afford to take a leap and make a change now, or in six months with some saving and cutting back on extras, or do you need to wait a year? Be practical and honest. When the time is right, hand in your notice with plenty of grace and a total lack of drama. Do not burn any bridges. I'm constantly amazed at how people from my past pop up in various roles, with different powers – people I first met over 20 years ago. And I'm always grateful, when we reunite in some professional or even personal capacity, that I never became an unreliable, unprofessional ass. Please don't. Resign politely, saying 'thanks for the opportunity', and keep dialling in for as long as your contract demands, acting with decorum to the end – not stealing anything, be it clients or a stapler. At your leaving do, don't slag off the boss. Life is pretty weird and you might be asking them for a job again one day.

Starting a new job is tricky, even when it comes with a better salary and prospects and a fresh start away from colleagues or bosses who didn't see your potential. Awkwardness around asking where things are, how things are done, and a new office culture, can throw you off for a bit. It takes six months to get totally to grips with a new position, but start yourself off in the right way by following these guidelines: be polite and friendly, but don't be too nosy and certainly don't jump into and take sides in office politics, gangs or dramas; keep your head down and focused on your role, while maintaining good manners; being civil and conservative in all matters should be your new job mantra; ask work-related questions and make generic small talk, but don't overshare, over-enthuse, overwhelm, or talk about how hellish your last job was or show off about what you achieved while you were there – don't say how brilliant you are, *show* it; let the praise come to you when it is earned rather than dragging it in with you; stay away from politics, parenting and religion; don't form opinions of your colleagues on day one – sometimes the ones who seem cooler towards you (even slightly suspicious) are the ones you'll become besties with in the end; start social interactions in a low-key way, asking where the best place is for coffee, meetings or lunch – a bit more social interaction and bonding might occur when they offer to take you.

Certainly, don't keep everything in at work all day, then let it all out on social media – use these public channels judiciously. And please, please, no arse-licking. Let your work and general all-round great vibes make you an integral part of the office, not how low down you can bow to the people in charge.

Turn your world upside down: get inverted

Recently, I was having one of those mornings when I didn't have the energy to be anything but my truest, most bare self – I just needed to get through the day. Any mask I may have normally worn for the ease or comfort of others was so dislodged that when I walked into a yoga class and someone asked how I was, I burst into tears and told the small group of kind, trustworthy women that I was feeling worn down. I'd had a fight with my husband,

I had a headache, a family member was going through some terribly sad shit, I was still processing the loss of a very dear friend, so I just didn't have the energy to put on a show. I felt safe in this space, and knew my worries would go no further, or be shared beyond our tight circle. Amazingly two things occurred: the other women in the small group all shared their anxiety and work worries, and we felt closer as we shared advice and support, and my yoga teacher offered a practical change we could make to our day. 'We're going to have a masterclass in inversions – we all clearly need it. The physical action of a headstand, shoulder-stand, handstand – or simply putting your legs up the wall – not only gets the blood flowing and endorphins rushing, which boosts a low mood, but seeing the world from a different angle literally gives you a new perspective.' We spent a large chunk of the next hour upside down and, I know it sounds too good (and simple) to be true, but I promise you, it helped.

Putting a ring on it

Getting married is a huge psychological change. We assume that if we know someone, love someone, live with someone, and perhaps parent with someone, that the legal bit of paper doesn't mean much. I found the opposite – in positive and negative ways. Don't underestimate the change that you will feel about your future, your rights, your security, your given name and your identity after you walk up the aisle. If I could offer you one piece of advice when contemplating this change, it would be this: don't focus on the day, focus on the life.

A wedding is wonderful, but that's just a few hours you are committing to. If things about your chosen one annoy you now, imagine them when you haven't had any sleep for days because you've got a newborn, and the burning flame of red-hot desire has died down into comforting embers after years together, and work is pulling you in demanding and different directions. It's easier to change your mind before the big day than after. I've had a few friends cancel their weddings at the eleventh hour, and as brutal and shocking as it is in the moment, they have all told me later that it made the mess a lot easier to clean up.

Enough of the negativity. Marriage can be great. It's lovely to feel bonded and unbreakable. Just be aware of some of the changes that can seep into wedlock: you'll argue more because you can (neither of you can run away so easily), you'll become a family (you'll be expected at more of his second cousin's kid's birthday parties), other people will ask you constantly about when you're having children (you can answer or ignore them) – and you will have erotic dreams about ex-partners, have panic attacks that you're trapped, have nightmares that your partner will die and you'll be left alone, and after planning your perfect wedding you'll be so bored you'll desperately look around for other big changes to make, such as a new home, new baby, new job, new hairdo, new lover – which is normally a mistake. Sit back and enjoy this big change before jumping into anything else.

Divorce as a decluttering tool

No one goes into a marriage wanting it to end, but when one or both of you are desperately unhappy, a change in marital status is not only inevitable but a necessity if you want to live an authentic, happy life. Two years ago, I witnessed my friend Gabriella go through a huge life change that she hadn't seen coming when she married her college sweetheart a decade before.

Although she wanted to split up, she still had to endure a period of mourning for the life she had once supposed she would have and what she had chosen to take away from her children. But alongside the grief was liberation. 'Sometimes life circumstances demand a declutter,' she told me. 'In my late thirties, I dealt with the sudden death of my father, a divorce from my only relationship since age 18, the switching of jobs, a move, all while juggling the co-parenting of two kids under six.' In survival mode, she found herself turning down invitations that she might have accepted before out of a sense of obligation or habit, a change she benefited from. She also changed her environment and her requirements. 'When I moved out of my marital home, I only took photographs and clothes. I didn't fight for shared items because I couldn't be bothered with things and I wanted to start afresh. I have found myself rebuilding myself, my surroundings and my priorities. The friends who really supported me through this tough time are dearer to me than ever. But I've also made new close friends who accepted me and the "mess" I was at that time. I've picked up hobbies I missed as a child and I've found brand-new interests as an adult. My house is now filled with my kids (and their stuff, which can always use another good purge) and only things that I love, as is my life.' Divorce is a blank page, startlingly and scarily empty at first, but whether you asked for it or not, it does force you to make a change, to find a love that deserves your love.

Tunes for change

Here are ten tracks to help you ride the tides of change in all its ups and downs, highs and lows:

- 'I Won't Give Up' by Jason Mraz
- 'Waiting on the World to Change' by John Mayer
- 'Landslide' by The Chicks
- 'A Change Is Gonna Come' by Sam Cooke
- 'Breakaway' by Kelly Clarkson
- 'Changes' by Ziggy Marley
- 'I'm Coming Out' by Diana Ross
- 'Laughter Lines' by Bastille
- 'Night Changes' by One Direction
- 'Stairway to Heaven' by Led Zepplin

Becoming a parent

'You know what parenting is?' a friend said to me recently. 'Parenting in this day and age is about loading your plate with 99 problems, getting wound up and stressed, while knowing that 86 of them are completely made up scenarios that will never happen.' It was true. Modern parenting has turned us into overanxious teachers, taxi drivers and entertainers, helicoptering over our offspring, fearful of what they do and worried about how others will judge us. This self-flagellation needs to change. Becoming a parent is probably the biggest change we can go through as a human, and of course it is scary, but it is also fun and beautiful. How can you embrace the change a child brings without falling apart? Don't engage in the 'I'm busier than you' game, competing over who has the most parties, sports classes or homework assignments on their calendar. We're all busy; we all have different coping mechanisms. There is no glory in taking on too much.

A recent survey of 2,000 Belgian parents published in the *Frontiers in Psychology* journal discovered that 12.9 per cent of mothers were suffering with 'high burnout', leaving them exhausted, less productive and emotionally withdrawn at least once a week. Instead of celebrating the martyrdom of burnout, something I've noticed more and more in my conversations in person and online with other mothers, reject it and correct it. Just because you're not as busy as other mothers say they are, it doesn't mean that you're not working as hard or that you are not as needed or as popular. It means that you are using your best judgement: saying no to unnecessary events or demands, prioritising sleep and self-care, refusing to engage in the 'I have such high expectations' game and quietly going about your business. Your children don't need a superhero. They need a mum. Put yesterday's drama behind you. Put the tantrum from five minutes ago behind you – yours or theirs! If you feel that you have something to apologise to your children for, explain and say sorry, think about why you did what you did, then move on. Don't let it worm away at your brain so that you then feel compelled to overcompensate or let them get away with things they shouldn't.

Make IOUs with mates you can trust, swap one school drop-off for a pick-up, take it in turns to buy joint teacher gifts, set a regular play-date schedule that gives you and your mum-friend a few extra hours of peace, babysit each other's kids so that you can have a date night with your partners without breaking the bank. We all have bad days; some are downright awful. When I have one of those, I take a pause. I break away from what has driven me mad or weakened me. Grab some fresh air, call a good friend, take a shower, or watch a favourite comedy clip on YouTube (Michael McIntyre on parenting will make you feel less ridiculous). And I accept that this is a road bump but that people have it far worse, and I look around to see what I can do to help someone else, something that will help my helplessness by making a positive difference, even if it's just sending a supportive text to a friend who is dealing with something difficult, sharing a friend's new business page on social media or donating to a cousin's fun run. Even small gestures make everyone feel better. And as you're tucking your kids into bed at night, ask them, if they're old enough, or ask yourself as their parents: 'What am I grateful for today?' You will find something meaningful that might not have occurred to you. Ask 'What am I excited about for tomorrow?' You will look forward to something that will make your mood lift and help you do all this parenting stuff again tomorrow.

Not becoming a parent

You don't have to procreate – and don't listen to anyone who tells you it is selfish of you not to. What *is* selfish is having a child and not giving it the love, care and attention it deserves. Parenting is hard, and not something to be taken on because you're responding to societal pressure to toe the 2-point-4-children line. A 2016 study on the effects of parenting on an adult's happiness published in the *American Journal of Sociology* discovered that parenting can be a mixed blessing for couples, bringing greater anxiety, depression and marriage dissatisfaction than their peers without children. Make the decision based on your dreams, desires and capabilities.

Getting real: Clara, 35

'The best piece of advice I've ever received as a mother was that parenting doesn't have to be perfect, just good enough. I often remind myself of that when I survey the playground on World Book Day with children in wonderful homemade costumes of literary characters, and mine are in their animal onesies which double as pyjamas by night. Or when I don't contribute homemade cakes to sell at the bake-off fundraiser. As a full-time working mum, I don't have time. Or rather, I choose not to make time for this, but the trick is to not feel guilty. Giving my children a few pounds to buy cakes at said fundraiser is an important part of participating too.'

Allowing your parents to become grandparents

They still love you, but everything is different now. They're getting older, as are you, so your relationship naturally changes, and then you add your children and it becomes a whole new world. Grandparents are brilliant, most of the time, loving your children as much as you do and helping you to care for them. Set expectations and guidelines around this multi-generational relationship to limit friction and misunderstanding. Remember to focus on the change in a positive way, at least initially. Grandparents interfere because they care. Don't be too defensive about every suggestion they make. Choose your battles. My mother tells me that she still sees me as her baby, and she wants to protect me, which sometimes can come across as telling me what to do, but always from a place of love. Don't boss them around. If your parents don't follow your rules about napping, sugar and television once a month when they're giving you a free-babysitter date night, don't chew them out. Remind them of your wishes in a non-confrontational way after the event, politely and gently. Your child will survive, but if you don't take this route, your relationship and cheap babysitting service may not.

Don't diss them in front of their grandchild. They're watching and picking up on how parents interact with their children, and vice versa from you lot – you're their role models. When big lines have been crossed, calmly take the grandparents to one side and ask for their support. Explain that you know that they are acting with love but that a certain expectation is important to you. If you catch them again, don't give up. Confront them, calmly, again and say that it's a real deal breaker for you and you're politely asking them to stop. If they refuse, you'll have to rearrange your relationship to maintain a bond that doesn't allow them a free hand with things that are important to you. Invite them along to play dates so that they can hear from other parents, buy them modern grandparenting books, email them relevant articles that you've enjoyed that reflect your expectations. Don't preach, just provide opportunities for them to set new rules. But don't dismiss their years of hands-on experience raising kids. After all, you turned out all right, didn't you?

If you don't feel your parents are interested enough, provide opportunities for them to foster relationships external to you. Perhaps nurture your child's love of gardening to fit in with your dad's weekend pastime, and ask if they could spend the afternoon together doing what they both love. Encourage your child to phone them regularly, or paint pictures for them that you can pop in the post. Remember, it's been a while since they've been around little ones – perhaps they are unsure, or scared of getting it wrong, or perhaps they're just tired. Be honest and speak up: tell them you'd love them to have a meaningful relationship and ask for their suggestions of how they could spend some quality time with the children.

This all applies to your in-laws, too. Don't be afraid to ask them to change something if you think you'd handle it better or quicker, or with fewer fireworks, than your partner, but give them the benefit of the doubt, too. Most grandparents are big fans of their grandkids.

Getting real: Charlotte, 30

'When my husband reached a very low point with his mental health, I bore the brunt of his anger over what was happening. Once the proper interventions took place, and he was back on course to being the lovely man that I fell in love with, he didn't have much of a memory of what that episode looked like, but I desperately wanted him to make it up to me and acknowledge the pain he had caused. I started taking some much-needed guided meditation classes and it clicked. Once I changed my attitude and chose joy, I realised that my husband was making more of an effort to connect with me. Once I relaxed, he relaxed and felt more accepted by me, so his guard started coming down. It was magical. I have managed to take stock of my feelings and the root cause much more quickly. I am convinced this changed the trajectory of our marriage. I could keep on resenting and keeping score of some biased imaginary game, or choose joy. The latter washed over me and I often bubble up inside with how much better this feels.'

Journal your journey – changes

Going through big changes can feel discombobulating and disconcerting: one minute you're buzzing with opportunity, the next you're wondering if you've made a terrible mistake.

Keep an eye on how you're handling it by noting down positive and negative emotions in a journal, alongside the things that quieten your mind and make you feel upbeat. You might feel more capable or self-assured at different times of the month, too, so keep a note of your hormones and how you've been sleeping and eating. Knowledge is power.

The change: handling the perimenopause

A weird thing has happened to me and my friends over the last year. Our authentic banter has gone to a new level: all small talk and slow-paced social niceties have gone out the window. On the infrequent nights that we actually get out to spend time together, away from our offices, small children and husbands, we delve straight into what is making us happy. And more importantly, as we all hover around our late thirties and early forties, what isn't. Never was this more obvious than a few months ago when I met some dear friends, four women I hadn't seen for 12 months. We didn't gossip about others, moan about partners, or analyse Kate Middleton's perennial sunniness. There were bigger issues on our minds. I asked for advice on dealing with a newly sprouted blonde moustache. Nicola shared that she could only muster the enthusiasm to have sex with her husband every other month and felt increasing alarm that she didn't miss the physical connection that once kept her marriage interesting. Lara unloaded her disappointment that after surviving two pregnancies – one with twins – her tummy had started to slide towards her kneecaps despite the extra effort she was putting in to crunch and plank daily.

We swapped tales of sleepless nights when, wracked with a strange heart-pumping panic, we'd lie awake worried about something so insignificant that only a few years earlier it wouldn't have even registered for a second thought: a funny look from a neighbour, a badly worded email from a child's teacher, watching an episode of *Last Tango in Halifax*. Anything, it appeared, would have us up all night, sweaty and disturbed.

'I guess that's just the life stage we're in now,' said Melissa. 'We have young children and we're juggling motherhood with work, and trying to maintain a relationship and a social life, and look somewhat decent. No wonder we're all paranoid about our appearance and feeling stressed and exhausted.'

Lara countered that this catalogue of unsettling symptoms wasn't purely circumstantial but medical too. She'd been to see her doctor the week before. 'We're perimenopausal, ladies. Our bodies are going through big changes, only exacerbated by our current situations.'

'What? I'm only 44 years old,' I replied. 'I've got a decade before all that starts.'

'You're thinking of menopause,' she replied. 'I'm talking perimenopause, which starts up to ten years before you actually stop having periods and have officially gone through the menopause. You're the demographic. You're not as young as you think you are.'

Lara emailed me the next day to apologise for being harsh. 'You meant well, no worries,' I replied. She had been up all night worried that she had upset me, obviously, because she was perimenopausal. 'It's just your peri-anxiety. What fun it is!'

It seemed that we were all in this huge life edit together. But what was it?

'Perimenopause means "around the time of menopause", when the ovaries' function begins to be reduced and women may start to have symptoms such as hot flushes, sweats, changes in periods, mood disturbance, vaginal dryness, decreased libido and difficulty sleeping,' explains Dr Ali Abbara, academic clinical lecturer in endocrinology at Imperial College London, when I ask him for the lowdown. So, the perimenopause is real? My friends and I aren't just suddenly feeling rubbish due to trying circumstances? 'It can sometimes be difficult to differentiate between symptoms which are specifically due to the hormonal changes of menopause and those which are coincidental to the time of menopause,' Dr Abbara writes. 'But it is widely accepted in the medical community that symptoms in the lead-up to menopause are both genuine and troublesome and are due to the changes in hormones as the ovaries cease to function.'

I found this information helpful in two ways. Firstly, I wasn't going mad. The changes I felt were valid and could be scientifically explained. I wasn't lacklustre in a self-imposed vacuum and my symptoms wouldn't continue to get worse and worse interminably. My medical manifestations had a time frame and an end date. Secondly, I now knew that I wasn't alone. Not only were my friends experiencing similar maladies and worries, but my entire peer group would be too, if not now, then soon. There was a collective consciousness about this change, and sharing thoughts and worries around it honestly would only help, I realised. Once I understood why I was feeling these things, from jet lag-like tiredness, to crying fits, to irrational worry, I knew I could get through it.

Self-awareness and appreciating we are part of a collective whole, a community, is powerful, and as my friends and I shared information, we felt more in control over our minds and bodies. We talked openly about this pre-change part of our life and gladly swapped advice on what to expect and what could help: weekend walks in nature and morning meditation to deal with anxiety, Bach's Rescue Sleep Remedy and no caffeine after midday for insomnia, a fan and a cotton nightie for the hot sweats. Authentic conversations with your doctor, armed with this knowledge around perimenopause, will help you decide when, and if, hormone replacement treatment is needed. Knowing that I have HRT as a back-up if my symptoms get too bad – and that the medical community understand this time in a woman's life better than they did when my mother was going through it a couple of decades ago – has reduced my anxiety about my perimenopausal anxiety, making me peri-normal again, much to the relief of everyone who lives with me as I go through this huge life change.

Own your story – here's how

It's time to check in and take stock of your desired changes, how long you want to give yourself to carry them out, and what you're hoping these changes will bring to your life.

Avoiding reality

Do you need to make a major life change that you've been putting off? Appraise your true story – your true self.

Use what you've got

Take hold of a landmark birthday, make a wish list or jot down New Year's resolutions to look at your life and what can be changed to improve your future – the next year, or the next decade.

Take your time

What's the rush? Plan, don't panic. Can you build a time frame that works? Have you got the money to do what you want to right now or should you save a little first?

Hang on to your end game

With any major life change, obstacles arise, challenges assault. Remind yourself what your goal is whenever you're knocked off course.

Enter the dragons

Your positive, dynamic changes will really annoy some people. Being your best, motivated self, taking on big tasks and making them happen, is going to make them feel insecure about where they are right now. Ignore them. Or tell them to join you. But stay focused on your truth.

Next steps matter

Don't get so caught up on one goal that you let other areas slide, or feel a depressive slump when it is achieved. When you're near to completing a move or task, set up a reward or the next healthy challenge.

▶

*T*ake stock

Listen to your head and heart before the change, during and when it has been made. What have you learnt about your personal strengths and weaknesses? What would you do differently?

*I*mplement the lessons you've learnt across your life

You planned and pursued these changes, and the experience of this can help you to cope with the unplanned ones. As Lao Tzu wrote: 'Life is a series of natural and spontaneous changes. Don't resist them; that only creates sorrow.'

*C*ongratulate yourself

Enjoy the fact that you went for something, or you were presented with something you didn't ask for and you saw it through. That takes courage, perseverance and a big, whopping dose of self-awareness.

Chapter 6

The Power of the People

'Be who you are and say what you feel, because those
who mind don't matter, and those who matter don't mind.'

Bernard M. Baruch

Last weekend, a dear friend organised a surprise celebratory
dinner for her husband's fortieth birthday. On his entrance,
we were to jump out and yell 'Surprise!' from behind a bamboo
wall in a hot new dim-sum spot in East London. With a strict
no-kids-allowed policy in place, my husband and I were looking
forward to an en masse date night catching up with people we
loved but rarely got to see. Our group of 16 was to be seated
along a long trestle table in the centre of the loud, flatteringly
lit restaurant, and as I saw my host-friend start to point at
people and tell them where to sit, plucking individuals into
an intriguing mix, I uncharacteristically rebelled. 'I never
get to talk to you without being interrupted by one of our
kids,' I whispered to my friend Carrie, 'I'm sticking with you.'

I wedged my bottom onto the bench next to her just as I was being beckoned towards a group of the birthday boy's (I'm sure lovely) university friends and advertising colleagues. I grinned and shook my head, cementing myself to my stolen slot. I felt a bit naughty and I certainly wasn't playing the role of the perfect guest, but I wanted to hear how Carrie had been, make sure she was OK, catch up on her work adventures. I weighed up the positives and negatives for standing my ground, and I cemented my derriere to the spot.

You see, until recently, I'd have allowed myself to be plonked into a group of sweet strangers, all charming and interesting, of course – just unknown, and spent my rare free time making small talk and asking them questions, knowing I'd probably never see them again. 'What do you do? Where do you live? Have you watched *Tiger King*?' And I'm over all that. There are millions of lovely people out there, but I've now realised that I don't need to know all of them.

Maintaining social connections and friendships is hard in our busy times; now I grab every opportunity to check in, enjoy and bolster the people I am invested in in the long term. That probably makes me a party pain-in-the-arse, but life really is too short to hear about a random guy's home security system. I prefer to cut to the chase, work in deep and meaningfuls, and halt unnecessary social interactions that don't nourish my soul. I've stopped saying yes to being that woman who always takes one for the team, because we should cut back on a lot of things, but spending time with people you love isn't one of them. An essay published by the Mayo Clinic explains how good friends improve self-confidence and self-worth and help get you through a trauma such as divorce, illness or the death of a loved one – or even just a bit of a slump or a bad day at work or with your children.

Fine-tuning your friendships

When life gets busy or fraught, time with friends is often the first thing to be edited out of our diaries. These crucial relationships are sent to the back of the queue while other things push their way to the front. Perhaps we allow this because we know that our peers are the ones who understand the life stage that we're in. They'll forgive our inaction when our boss or child won't – but should we forgive ourselves? As a wealth of information linking loneliness and depression emerges, so should our focus on maintaining meaningful connections. Friends help you to create a life you love, a life that you can cope with.

A study published in the journal *PLOS Medicine* highlights how social isolation can be as bad for your health as smoking or obesity. When we feel supported by good friends, another study shows, our blood pressure lowers, we have a stronger immune system and we display better hormone function. Authentic friendships need to be cherished, not edited out.

We need different friends for different moments and different stages in our lives, there is no such thing as the perfect friend with all the answers to everything. We need the friends who help us build and maintain healthy habits, the friends who we can download our family or work upsets onto without fear of judgement, the friends who celebrate our successes, the friends who help our lives go smoothly. We need old friends to keep us authentic and new friends to help us change. We need friends that we can care for and friends who will look after us. If you have someone in your life who doesn't do any of this, consider why you've allotted them a place in your heart and calendar? As a wise woman said to me recently, when I was hurt that a social date between three friends wasn't rearranged to include me, 'If your absence doesn't bother these friends, your presence never bothered them either.' Ouch! That truth hurt. Make time and show love to those who value you. Never allow yourself to feel insignificant in someone's life, especially when you have made them too significant in yours.

Friends who hold their value

Invest into the friendship bank that offers:

- A good rate of return: friends who are consistently positive grow your emotional stock and boost your health reserves.
- Twenty-four-seven hours: friends who make time for you, who you can count on around the clock – if not physically, which is often impossible, but you know they are there supportively.
- Great customer service: friends who respond to your emails, texts and invites, who check in with you to make sure you're doing OK when you're going through something, who make you feel good about decisions.
- Sound advice: friends who are worth listening to, who offer interesting suggestions.

- Opportunities: friends who allow you to try new things and explore new areas.
- A quiet lobby to wait in: a safe space, a warm place where you can sit doing nothing and saying nothing but feel perfectly at peace.

How to be a better friend

If your friend game needs to be raised, get revising and revamping your matey modus operandi ASAP. Authentic friendships are invaluable, offering the warmth of family without the obligation, guilt or tumultuous history. Research by a team at the University of Virginia uncovered that when someone walked, carrying a heavy rucksack, with a friend, as opposed to walking alone, hills felt less steep and arduous and the load felt lighter. Closeness physically helps us to move and to motivate – and we feel that a burden is lighter.

How can you edit your own behaviour to become a better friend and keep hold of those dear ones who lighten your mental load? You can: offer logistical support when they're going through a tough, busy time (help with errands, drop off food, coffee or treats, look after their children for an afternoon); offer a laugh – force them to go to the cinema with you, or send them a comedy clip or podcast; apply some positive peer pressure – if they're feeling frumpy or low, encourage them to walk with you, or try a healthy-eating challenge, or sign up for a free trial at a local gym; and be active in their lives – checking in when you know they're dealing with something nasty, and celebrating with them when something wonderful has happened. Don't just rely on news via social media. Check in on a personal, private level from time to time, they're not sharing *everything* with the world; schedule dates and stick with them – don't be the flake who always cancels at the last minute or shows up late. Show them that you value everything about them, including their time.

Editing friendships when they need some work: a cautionary tale

Claire had always been in my life. My mother remembers our first meeting as toddlers, dressed by chance in similar dungarees (a mainstay of the stylish 70s child) and shiny, patent shoes, playing happily together on a cake-icing high at her cousin's birthday party. I can't recall much about our days of free milk and sports days at our East London infant and junior school, but I've seen the photos of us, summer after summer, glumly posing in green gingham dresses for annual class portraits, snapped on the lawn where we normally played chase. Our friendship deepened into sisterhood during sixth form.

When my grandmother died suddenly when I was 16, we bunked off school and Claire smuggled me into her house to mollycoddle me with a duvet, a viewing of *My Girl* and beans on toast. Her mother worked, whereas mine stayed at home with my baby brother, so she knew I'd be safe there without a concerned parent telling us we must dry our tears and return to economics class. When I failed my driving test at 17, Claire picked me up in her dad's hatchback, eyes glassy with empathy, and handed me a cassette tape of 'Everybody Hurts' by REM. She told me that she knew, undoubtedly, that I'd pass next time – which I did.

At 18, when a spiteful popularity contest led our bigger friendship group to combust and dismantle, despite feeling devastated and confused I never felt alone because Claire was also left standing outside this newly formed social circle, and I knew Claire wouldn't let me down. Instead of focusing on the mean girls at school, we discovered an exciting new world of cappuccinos, cocktails and Oscar Wilde quotes and turned into a couple of runaways, desperate to escape the Essex suburbs our parents had dragged us to in our pre-teens for the bright lights of London. We spent our weekends catching the Central Line, headed west, towards our dreams: lives of romance, success and independence; lives we thought, with the naiveté and bravado of youth, would come easily to us both, simultaneously. Through university, we stayed just as close, although 100 miles apart. When she backpacked in Australia for a year after graduation, while I started work at *Marie Claire*, I flew out to Sydney for two weeks to comfort her when she said she was homesick.

It was when she returned to London and we decided to rent a place together that we had the first problems in our 22-year relationship. Our Blackheath home became a hotbed for female frustration and the insecurities that swell when some are seemingly doing better than others. As I struggled to gain respect in journalism for a pittance, she was fighting chauvinism in banking but earning an impressive amount. We were both working long hours for difficult bosses, and instead of consoling each other, we took our stress and uncertainty and flung it in barbed comments at the other one's feet. Our authentic personalities were being disguised by the masks we were now wearing to fit in with people in our chosen industries. And our personal lives were changing, too. As I settled down into the first serious romance of my life, Claire was enjoying her freedom. Or at least she looked as if she was. Deep down, we were both so desperate to forge the perfect adult lives we'd dreamed of as teenagers that we ignored warning bells: I had massive concerns about my new man, but was too insecure to escape for fear that this was my only shot, while Claire, looking outside-in on my date nights and Valentine's Day gifts, imagined I was the lucky one. But instead of doing what we had always done, talk to each other openly and kindly – authentically – we bickered and bitched (and I was the worst by far) until Claire moved out. Suddenly, she was not there any more.

We didn't speak for 18 months. I handled it at first, pumped up by foolish pride and indignation, yet a year on I was depressed. I'd grown up imbibing the belief that men come and go but women are in your life for ever. I was raised by my mother, grandmother and three aunts, all of whom had suffered heartbreak and divorce, and who had learnt the hard way that without good women around a tough life is even tougher. I had been taught from birth that women need to encourage and value each other, and yet here I was, failing at my first grown-up test of friendship and female solidarity. I missed everything about Claire but was too scared to pick up the phone, or show up at her office, which could backfire publicly, and because of the beaten-down ego I was sporting, thanks to the boyfriend, I wouldn't have been able to handle it. Had she cut me out of her life for good? Had I been edited out of Claire's adulthood?

Authoring change

There are times in our lives when we need to rewrite our story and choose a happier ending for ourselves. Thinking about this when I thought of Claire, a plot twist came to mind. A letter! A letter could help to rebuild the bridge. We'd cherished the weekly letters we sent to each other during our first year at university and I knew her well enough to know she wouldn't be able to resist reading it. This letter turned out to be the most important piece of writing of my life. More than 20 years later, I can still say that. I remember my vulnerability as I sat alone at my desk on a concrete-grey autumn day in front of a blank piece of paper and tried to think of everything I wanted to tell her, desperate tears weaving down my cheeks to my neck, splashing my pen. I have the most appalling handwriting, so as I started to write, I tried to slow down and neaten my scrawl, desperate for Claire to be able to read every honest word that tumbled out from my broken heart onto the pale yellow stationary. I reminded her of the good times: the complaints our school received from angry parents after our raunchy dance recital when Claire took it upon herself to freestyle a bump and grind floor routine during the final notes of George Michael's 'Too Funky', pretending to study for our A-levels while sunbathing on the beach in North Norfolk and reciting Lord Byron into the sand dunes, the drunken kisses with boys from the local private school who had all the floppy hair of Hugh Grant but none of his nervousness, our ghost-hunting trips around the Essex countryside that left our gangly limbs buckling and covered in goosebumps. I shamelessly tickled her funny bone and pulled at her heartstrings.

'I love you, I miss you and I'm so very, very sorry,' I wrote. 'Spending 18 months of my life without you has made me realise that pride is a cold, cold quality next to the warmth of an old friend, and I don't want to spend one more day without you. I don't know who I was trying to be when we fell out, but it wasn't the real me.'

I concluded my letter asking if she would meet me on neutral ground, a quiet wine bar we both knew, in one of those ramshackle lanes next to St Paul's Cathedral. Essentially, I'd written her a love letter and asked her for a date. I have not, to this day, written anything so filled with desperate devotion to a man. I had found out the hard way that the love we feel for friends can be just as powerful as the love we feel for a romantic partner and that breaking up with a best friend is sometimes worse than breaking up with a boyfriend, because we need our best friends to get us through those times. I'd poured my soul onto the packed sheet of paper and posted it off to her parents' suburban address along with my heart. Waiting for her reply was excruciating. She had every right to say no, I knew, but I was praying that I could count on her perennially sweet nature and rational mind – and I convinced myself that she *must* miss me as much as I missed her. She did. Eight days later, I instantly recognised her bouncy vowels when her reply dropped through my letter box. As my heart hammered in my chest, I ripped open the envelope. She said yes! She would meet me – the following Thursday at 6.30pm, at the bar in St Paul's I'd suggested.

Opening our communication again via letters allowed our reunion to be calm. Getting our emotions, explanations and apologies out on paper before meeting face to face was a sensible idea. It allowed us to discuss briefly the sentiments in our letters rather than the drama that went before it, before moving on and catching up on the present. After an hour, we were holding hands, verbally supporting each other in new endeavours – as we always had done before moving in together – and crying happy tears into our giant glasses of Chianti. I had my best friend back. Now in our forties, with the social and emotional skills to deal with upsets and dilemmas more authentically, I am forever thankful that I found the courage to Tipp-Ex over my ego, edit my misbehaviour and say no to letting her go.

Why it's healthy for you to apologise

Saying sorry and owning your mistakes is more than a social ritual to placate ill feeling; it is a chance to press the reset button on a relationship that has gone awry. It can soothe the mind of both the person being apologised to and the person apologising, removing unspoken anger, upset and resentment – on both sides. For the giver of the apology it can:

- Reduce the damaging emotions of guilt and shame, allowing us to rebuild self-esteem and self-respect.
- Instil a humility that is much needed in social inter-actions, giving a lesson in courage and grit, and helping us to develop diplomacy skills.
- Rebuild important relationships that we don't want to jeopardise. Feeling guilty about our words or actions towards someone pushes up an invisible wall, making communication impossible.

Apologising is such a difficult act to do, just the simple task of doing it should put us off behaving stupidly or cruelly again, making us better people in the future.

How to say sorry

You need to show genuine remorse for your words or actions. You need to acknowledge how your choices caused hurt, whether it was intentional or not. No one is perfect, but we can own our blame, listen to the injured party and move forward:

- Start simple. 'I'm sorry.' Be authentic in your choice of words – be honest with yourself and the other person about your regret without making the apology about you. You are not looking for sympathy; you are attempting to set your bad behaviour straight.
- Give power to the other person's feelings. Put yourself in their shoes and apologise not only for your part in it directly, but also how you may have made them feel afterwards over the subsequent days. They may have felt embarrassed, ridiculed and so on. Own your part in that.
- Don't excuse yourself – that will lessen the impact. This is about making amends, it's not about forcing them to listen to you go on about your day, your drama. Making excuses will just push them into a weird position of wondering if they should be apologising to you or feeling sorry for you.

- Make peace with intent. 'How can I make it up to you?' 'Can I do anything to show you how sorry I am?' Offer them a show of peace – to an appropriate level. Don't offer them your firstborn.
- Give them your guarantee. This was a one-off. You're not generally an ass. You've reflected on your behaviour and they won't have to bear the brunt of it again.
- Don't expect normal service to resume immediately. Even if they accept your apology, hurt and resentment can linger. Just move forward with kindness and humility ... and make sure it doesn't happen again.

Why it's healthy for you to accept an apology

Feeling wronged can have a physical effect on our bodies, making it hard for us to sleep, eat, concentrate and relax. Although when someone asks you to accept their apology you might feel as if it lets them off the hook, hearing them out will have a positive effect on you, too.

- Studies prove that receiving a sincere apology reduces blood pressure, slows heart rate and helps breathing.
- Acknowledging that everyone messes up sometimes allows you to accept that in yourself, too, allowing you to practise self-kindness and reflect on your own mistakes.
- It gives you a chance to learn about yourself: are you too stubborn, too prideful, what insecurities do you need to address to stop this kind of thing from hurting you again?

- Hearing an apology will allow you to quieten your emotions around a difficult issue. The olive branch is extended, and a soft blanket of acceptance can be laid across your anger.

How to forgive

Accepting an apology doesn't always equal forgiveness. Or perhaps you can forgive, but you can't forget. In an ideal world, a sincere apology would automatically lead to forgiveness and forgetting the upset, as it did when I apologised to Claire two decades ago, but every problem is different, and everyone's ability to move on is unique. Some things, after all, are truly unforgivable. If, however, you want to keep this person in your life – or you have to – there are some tips to making forgiveness a little easier:

Try not to let your negative bias take over and play tricks on you. Yes, this person has done something terrible – but was it all terrible? Have they actually helped you out, respected you, loved you and made your life easier in other ways, at other times? It is easy to focus your overall anger towards your whole history, not just the one indiscretion. If they have made one mistake, try to think of the times when they didn't. Write a list of their pros and cons if it helps.

If you can't forgive, look inwards, rather than focusing on the outside influences. What can you change about your own self-defence mechanisms and your ability to cope with trauma? Are you making a mountain out of a molehill? If you are, that is your right, but use this experience as a route to personal growth.

Take responsibility for your part in the drama Looking at the indiscretion from both sides, accepting your fair share of the blame, should make it easier to forgive.

Think about being kind instead of right We never know what other people are going through, or what they have had to endure to get them to where they are, with the views they have. Have faith in your good heart, and project kindness to those who have wronged you, rather than smugness or wrath.

Use common sense Are you too easily offended? Are you look-ing to be insulted? Stop it. Most people are just trying to make it through the day, thrown constantly by changing societal standards, rules and regulations. When considering whether to forgive someone or not, engage your brain and look at their motives: were they spiteful, or just misguided? Can they learn?

Journal your journey – friends

Open a blank page and make a list of the people who have really enthralled, excited and understood you – the different friends you've made across the years in different compartments of your life. As you read back each name, bathe in your magical memories and give thanks for what you shared. Then shift to the present. To live ▶

your happiest, truest life you should live in the moment, shrugging off the weight of bad memories or painful experiences. Edit out once and for all those people or things who offer no goodness, and move on from things in the past when you can. Write the names of people you love and cherish, and a list of people you need to let go of. Then cross through the negative names, wishing them well as you erase them from your life.

When someone shows you who they really are, believe them!

Saying no to friendships that don't serve your happiest self is one of the most important life edits that you can make. Sometimes friendships don't root, sprout and bloom in the way that we planned. Perhaps a person you had high hopes for turns out to be not on your level, or they don't have the time or the desire to develop a relationship with you. Perhaps someone you thought was cool soon starts to take over your happy place like a weed; perhaps you've noticed that they don't have a good word to say about anyone else, making you wonder what they say about you when you're not around. Perhaps your supposed friend has become your biggest critic; or you sniff a note of sourness whenever you share good news. Sometimes, things just don't gel and you find conversation a struggle. Accept it. We can't like all the people all the time – and sadly (I've found out the hard way) people won't always like us. It might be hard to work out what is going wrong, or how a promising relationship has become bitter, or if you're imagining the weird vibes, but if you don't feel relaxed, happy and confident in your relationship, you need to stop saying yes to time with this person, and move on.

How, then, do you edit your diary to increase space for people who do like you, the ones who make you feel enriched, excited and supported? Start with your feelings – the visceral, gut impulse that makes you feel *yes, this is healthy*, or *no, it isn't*. 'Stay close to people who feel like sunlight, companions who show you warmth and brighten your day. Don't waste time with those who pull you into darkness,' a life coach I met once told me, after I'd been disgruntled by a rude comment by someone I'd assumed would become a good friend. Her statement made sense instantly: think back to dates you've had with friends. With some, do you leave feeling light and free, warmed from your head to your toes? Keep them. With others, do you leave feeling confused about a statement, feeling misunderstood or nervous that you've done something wrong, but you can't be sure what? Cut them.

Sometimes, in any and all kinds of relationships, we behave badly – like I did with Claire. Make sure you're putting your own behaviour under scrutiny, too, but if you are faultless – or as near as dammit – and if you've given someone the benefit of the doubt for a time that feels right to you but it's not working, feel free to back off. The only way to win with a toxic person is not to play their game, so don't feel under pressure to spend your valuable spare time with someone who doesn't make you feel great. Some people, posing as friends, want to put you down, keep you down and make you feel down about yourself. These people aren't necessarily nasty, just human, and you need to raise your friend-selection game. And you need to know you have power to create the inner circle you desire: it is OK to unfollow people who do not feed your best self in real life, too, not just on social media.

Getting real: Annabel, 46

'Since turning 40, I have started to be more honest with myself about how I was being treated in my friendships. I realised that I gave everybody the same amount of love and energy, and I found it exhausting when I was misread and would then go into rabbit holes about how I could have done something differently, and so on. I learnt that no matter how good and honest my intentions were, I was never going to change crazy, for a lack of a better term. Some people see what they see, no matter what. The mere fact that someone was misreading me or thought my intentions were dubious would be so upsetting. For this reason, I devised a colour-coding system. I would think of a friend and then be mindful of how I felt. If I felt safe and happy, I mind-swiped them into the "green zone", if they are an acquaintance or friend that has given me pause, for whatever reason, I mind-swipe them into the "yellow zone" and if they have a proven pattern of crazy or hurtful behaviour, they are the "red zone" friends. It sounds ridiculous, but this simple colour-coding system has helped me to lean in on the "green" friends and create firmer boundaries with the reds and yellows.'

One more try ... and then goodbye

You must take control of a negative situation with a friend before it starts to eat away at your spirit. First, be upfront. Remind them that you are friends who are there to support each other, and if any of your changes have made them uncomfortable and distressed, rather than happy for you, you can talk about it. Self-improvement or moving into your power and authenticity can often bring out the worst in friendships – with one person becoming resentful of a positive change in the other, such as weight loss, a job promotion or finding new friends. Perhaps they could join you in your new positive attitude, rather than trying to bring you down. Perhaps you did something hurtful and you need to clear the air. This is your chance.

If the upfront approach doesn't work, or if it makes the situation worse, you need to respectfully back away. When you are editing your life for the better, you need to surround yourself with people who love you, not those who feel embittered with anger or aggression towards you. As you become more self-confident, positive and aware of your values, you will naturally attract friends who bolster you rather than knock you down.

If cutting them out feels too harsh, just take more control. See them when *you* want to, not when they demand to see you. Learn to say no. Switch off your phone if they're blowing it up. Block them from social media. Refuse to engage in negative talk about others. Stand up for yourself if you sense that they're trying to bully or criticise you, your choices or your loved ones. Spend more time with people who make you feel good. This friendship might still feel like a cross you have to bear, but at least you won't lose your self-respect. Next, you should learn the art of anti-stalking. Note a person's usual routine and hangouts so that you can avoid running into them. Ending friendships can be emotionally draining, so limit your upset – and theirs – by carefully and thoughtfully restricting interactions when possible. You need to safeguard your emotional well-being.

And if you're the one edited out . . .

If a friend you have treasured cuts you out of their life, look at their reasons and your actions with an authentic approach, a clear head and an open heart. If you find anything wanting within yourself, change it. Do you have a negative, repetitive flaw? Delete it. Become a better friend in the future. Project good vibes towards them and open up some space. If you know in your heart that you didn't do anything wrong, mourn the loss and move on. When I was not so subtly cut a few years ago, a clever mate reminded me, 'Don't feel sad over someone who gave up on you; feel sorry for them because they gave up on someone who would have never given up on them.'

Switching off your social life

Ah, social media! It was invented to make our world smaller and more deeply connected, but instead it quickly became an addiction tinged with popularity-contest vibes that we're all struggling to get to grips with. We love people, right? Most of us do, and we love to know what our friends are doing, how they are and what they're thinking. But for many of us now, staring at a phone and mistaking that for a true, meaningful social connection is taking away from more authentic, deep in-person relationships. We're losing the ability to pick up the phone and listen to someone's voice and we're forgetting to meet in person, assuming that we get all we need from our news feeds. Social media is here to stay, and we can use it to our benefit, but we do have to remember a cold, hard phone screen cannot replace the warmth of a hug, or eye-to-eye contact.

According to a 2017 survey, the average Brit checks their social media accounts on their phone 28 times a day. We're obsessed. That's once an hour, at least, and 10,000 times a year. Some of the posts we engage in are good, but some of them are very, very bad. The good things about keeping up with the world's shenanigans online are the feelings of connection it can give you to friends and family far away. Also, FOMO can be reduced, when you see how your niece's dance recital went or you get to wish your university chum a happy birthday and reminisce about the previous birthday fun you've had together. Social media allows sufficient anonymity that people can share problems or seek out others like them to discuss them with, which will alleviate a sense of loneliness and isolation. Social media can also be used as a motivational tool to live a healthier life. Following someone's journey as they lose weight, give up drinking or train for a 5k, or sharing your own goals, improves accountability and focus. At a more grass-roots level, social media can help you to learn about things that are happening in your area and put you in touch with like-minded people. But – and it's a huge, bright, blinking *but* – if we allow social media to replace real-life conversations, interactions or sleep, the effects on our mental health can be damaging.

Our brains get overloaded with perfectly filtered photos and other people's happy news, which can have a knock-on effect on our self-esteem. We can feel lesser and flat in comparison to these heavily edited and carefully curated words and images flashing before our eyes. In fact, a study by the University of Copenhagen found that 'Facebook envy' was a real phenomenon, and people who abstained from using Facebook reported feeling more satisfied with their lives. If someone is winding you up constantly, think about hiding their newsfeed, or even blocking them. Don't worry – they won't get an instant alert telling them what you've done. They may never work it out. Or consider checking out of your accounts for a while. You can easily take a month off, and when you realise how freeing it is – and how much free time you get back – you can continue without it or be more able to set firm restrictions moving forward. But just remember this: you wouldn't let a hurtful or harmful person into your home, and you don't have to let them in via your phone either. Take back control.

Social media is also having a detrimental effect on our social skills. For something that connects us, it also disconnects us from meaningful face-to-face quality time. It even stops us from picking up the phone. And it has a bad effect on your brain: we're spending so long online rather than being present that we're not absorbing life as it happens with our own eyes and emotions. It's also damaging our attention span. When there's easy, quick, constantly changing entertainment at our fingertips, our brains struggle to maintain focus throughout a film or play, or even a half-hour television show. It is making it harder for us to concentrate in all areas of our lives, without our fingers and minds twitching for bright, shiny social news. Most importantly perhaps for our health and well-being is what it does to sleep quality. The junk light from mobile devices suppresses the sleep hormone melatonin, and feelings of envy or anxiety can overstimulate our brains before bed, making it impossible to settle for the soothing night's sleep that we need.

Getting real: Zoe, 32

'If I ever go down a social media spiral, I remember what a wise friend told me. "It's not all real. It's a story they're telling themselves, that they want others to read and believe." His analysis is true. When you meet enough people that have a charming social media presence but are toxic in real life, it makes it easier to participate on those platforms. You know it is just a glimpse, what they want you to see. You're being manipulated, so just assume most of it isn't real anyway and engage on your terms with your logic and bullshit detector switched on.'

Say yes to social self-regulation

Here's how to step away from your screen to eliminate the negative side effects of social media and the devilish doings of devices:

- Beware of just how much of your life you're wasting staring at a screen. Make a note. Four hours? You could have gone to the cinema in that time, read half a great book, cleaned your whole house and had a bubble bath. Instead your brain is just buzzing with what other people have achieved. Being aware of the maths will keep you in check.
- Read a book or listen to a mediation app at bedtime, instead of staring at unsettling news or social show-offs. Try switching off an hour before bed. Go back to using an old-fashioned alarm clock if you're using that as an excuse for keeping your phone next to your bed. Invest in a book light so that you can read good literature and not scroll through depressing news stories online.
- Be strong and say goodbye to your phone. Don't take your phone on family walks. Don't have it on the dinner table. Don't take it into the bathroom with you. Leave it in the hotel room on holiday. If you use it as a camera – as I do, which I use as my excuse to have it with me at all times – buy a lightweight digital camera and sling that in your bag instead.
- Limit your data. You don't need to be up to speed on every social media platform at all times. Choose one you love, or commit to the one most of your favourite people are on, and ditch the rest. There's too much these days; edit out the ones that just wind you up and focus on the one that brings you the most joy.
- If you haven't got the willpower to power down your devices, set one up. There are programs that chuck you off social media platforms after your pre-set amount of

time. Or be strict and set social-media-free times in your house. We have set one that starts when the kids arrive home after school until their bedtime.

Own your story – here's how

It's time to check in and note, score and plan your most authentic life going forward; a life filled with people who love you, want you to be happy and appreciate you for who you are.

Analyse who deserves you

'Don't let wack-ass people mess with your cool-ass energy,' a friend told me recently after a relationship went sour. With an open heart, decide who is worth your time.

Use every minute

As your life twists and turns, you might not have spare time to spend on your friends, but do what you can. What small gestures can you make today? How can you check in? Show you care? A text, a quick hug at the school drop-off or after a meeting, a birthday card. Forward a joke, share a link, send good vibes. You can keep communications short – just keep it real.

Treat others how you would like to be treated

Value their time and energy. Don't let them down at the last minute, and don't gossip about them behind their back. ▶

*H*ave their back

Loyalty is a must, so defend them, listen to them, assume the best in them.

*E*ngage with people who pull the magic out of you

Avoid those who cause madness or mayhem.

*N*urture friendships that feed you

Devote as much love and attention to your core circle of friends as you would a romantic relationship. There is true love in real friendships.

*T*ell them what they mean to you

Hearing you are loved and valued never gets old; in person, an email, a letter. It can make someone's day to know that they are thought about kindly.

*I*nitiate new bonds

Don't be shy to reach out to someone you admire. They could need a new friend, too. Old friends are gold friends, but new friends can help you build a community in your current life, or get you through a new stage of life, career or dilemma.

*C*ut back on relationships that wear you out

A true friendship leaves you feeling appreciated, understood and supported. You are allowed to say no to people who take from you without giving. Energy vampires will not help you lead a life of authentic happiness; they'll suck you dry.

Chapter 7

Lead the Way, *Your* Way

'There are risks and costs to action. But they are far less
than the long-range risks of comfortable inaction.'

John F. Kennedy

You are the manager of your own life, deep down. You might
be buried under bills and responsibilities but you are your own
boss when it comes to digging down to set and maintain your
short- and long-term goals. Building a career is about more than
bringing in the pounds. Our professional life is connected,
rightly or wrongly, to our self-worth, social status and feelings
of purpose, so we have to make it work for us. Research con-
ducted by Harvard Business School uncovered that a scary 94
per cent of professionals spend more than 50 hours per week
working, with half of those counted racking up 65 hours per
week. I don't need to tell you that this means they're letting
the rest of the things that make them human – sleep, society,
replenishing alone time – slip away. This is not good for our
mental or physical health, or our happiness.

A recent British survey showed that the average adult spends 7,994 hours of their life dwelling on their regrets and wishing that they had taken more risks. If they had listened to their gut, 29 per cent believe that they would have been happier, and 17 per cent believe that they would be in their dream job. This is such a tragedy. When 44 per cent of the respondents admit that a fear of failure stops them from trying new things and reaching their true potential, it's clear that, as a society, we are following the wrong rules and valuing the wrong things, looking too much to what other people expect, with little regard for our precious hearts and personal needs – especially when it comes to our professional life.

The most successful ongoing life edit I have made to my professional life is to stop seeking validation in my career from those who are disinterested or disinclined to give it, regardless of my talent or hard work. I have to reset my head regularly, because its default position is to one of self-doubt. But it's imperative I do force myself to make these readjustments. Why? Because seeking approval from anyone other than your best, highest self is just a trap: a trap to make you feel unworthy or unimpressive, always on the push for more, more, more, which, it turns out, is never enough, never filling in the empty nooks and crannies that live within you. You need to build your career, your enthusiasm and your ambition on your own desires, economic needs and strengths – no one else's. Once you understand this, a weight will be lifted. You'll feel freer to pursue a life that makes you feel professionally and purposefully fulfilled, without worrying about being left behind or not being important enough. Choosing a career because your parents or your school push it on you, or continuing a career because that is what is expected of you, or you've been told to chase the money, won't make you happy – and since the average person spends a third of their day working, that makes for some pretty miserable living.

When it comes to our careers, we are often too willing to hand our autonomy to someone else: our boss, our colleagues, our bank manager, our partner. We blame others for our bad times and give them credit for the good. We dial down who we really are, we play a game that makes us feel itchy-scratchy at our core, we forget that there is life outside our corporate culture, away from our cohort or collegues, external to our industry or office building. All this makes it brutal when it falls apart, is taken away from us, or we are left behind. I know this too well. When I was 27, I was made redundant when a monthly magazine I was working for closed down. The whole team was gutted. We were in the flow, our work life spilling into our social lives and becoming a tangled web of everything each of us were as individuals. After the initial shock subsided, I remember it brought to the fore lots of unhelpful questions about myself: was I interesting without this great job title and access to the hottest, happening parties? Was I a good enough journalist to get another job, and quickly, because I had a mortgage to pay for?

Luckily, I got another job within a month, but, with hindsight, I wish I'd used those four weeks to actually think about what was good for me and what I needed, not worrying so much about what everyone else would think about me. I wish I'd appreciated then that I had self-determination and that this was an opportunity to reflect and revise my career path. Our fear around social standing is one of the big things that we need to repel: we need to stop saying yes to giving our power away. Our profession does feed into who we are, but it is not *all* we are.

Unless of course we create a life where that is what makes us the most fulfilled and we don't need anything else.

Fitting the pieces of the work–life puzzle

Learn to say no This is probably the biggest way to get balance. You don't have to attend every work happy hour, leaving party, conference or meeting. Delegation is power, self-care is strength. In a world of constant requests upon our time and energy, and the barrage of opportunities that we feel we have to take, take a minute to think about what you really must say yes to.

Think about what 'non-promotable' tasks you're taking on, especially if you're a woman. Females in the workplace are more likely than men to volunteer or say yes to unhelpful requests from higher up that do not serve our careers – things such as organising office whip-rounds for new babies, planning the Christmas bash or charity days. Before you say yes and overload yourself, consider whether this will actually help your career or hinder it by taking away your time.

Unplug Yes, we *can* be connected 100 per cent of the time now, but it doesn't mean that we *have* to be. Put an auto reply on your emails when you're on holiday which routes enquiries in a healthy direction, then put your phone on silent at an appropriate hour of your choosing each evening. Know that everything except a genuine emergency can wait – you need to decide what is important. A friend recently posted a message on her Facebook page and it really reminded me of the reality of this: 'We've already let our phones replace our watch, clock, camera, map and calendar – don't let it replace your friends and family.' Preach!

Have fun at work – this isn't impossible. Some of my heartiest guffaws have happened in my workspace. Volunteer yourself to a project if an idea floats your boat, learn new skills in new departments if you think they look interesting, take treats in to share, giggle about niggles rather than talking badly about people. Keep a check on your negative talk and gossip, and celebrate your colleagues' successes, both professional and personal.

Don't undersell your social or family time Put it in your diary so that it is not the first thing that is thrown under a bus when things get hectic. If you have children, spend time with them, and return to work once they're in bed. Spend a chunk of your weekend with them, then work while they're chilling with a movie or Lego set. Don't let worry about work creep into every aspect of your life. Face it head-on, with a plan, then forget about it. Focus on good results, rather than how much time you spend pinned to your desk.

Stop second-guessing yourself in a quest to be perfect. As genius writer Anne Lamott wrote, 'Perfection is shallow, unreal, and fatally uninteresting.' Even at work, a few mistakes or mishaps can bring interesting developments and ideas … and can stop you from having adrenal fatigue in your constant search for infallibility.

Practise self-care, even in the office. Get up and walk around once an hour, get some fresh air at lunchtime, chat to colleagues, try to eat well and drink enough water. Can you fit in a trip to the gym or a yoga class on a quiet day? Exercise is an effective stress reducer and endorphin booster, much needed during hectic work days, and yoga and meditation will calm down your parasympathetic nervous system, which helps us to rest, digest and stay calm. Can you tick off a few personal chores in a quiet moment so that you have more time to rest and switch off after work? Can you use your commute to listen to uplifting music or an inspiring non-fiction book, or take a quick tour of a new exhibition at the museum a brisk walk away when you force yourself to leave on time or, dare I say it, a few minutes early? All these little edits will help you to avoid burnout, balance your cortisol levels and help you to maintain emotional stability.

Don't look at the office as a prison, even if your office is in your home. Make your desk space work for you. Keep pretty, joyful things around to soothe your eyeballs, a scent to spray for a 60-second soul break. Invest in a comfortable chair, a support stand for your laptop, non-glare gadgets and an ergonomic keyboard. Think about teaming up with some colleagues to decorate the staff kitchen or lounge, too. Fill it with nice things to drink and a few magazines. If you do work from home, don't let the chaos of family life encroach on your workspace if you possibly can.

Understand how productivity and creativity go hand in hand
Allow yourself a long lunch break to take a walk or meet a friend every now and again. That's likely to promote more fresh

thoughts than a rushed sandwich at your desk. And schedule me time and creative time – or simply daydream time – into your calendar, too. This will rejuvenate and revamp your tired mind.

Have your personal *and* professional goals in your brain at all times. They are not necessarily the same thing. What do you hope for in work *and* life over the next month, year, decade? Note them down, adapt when you need to, use the list as motivation and as a way of remembering that you are not just a working robot, you have personal priorities that run alongside your career.

Don't get caught up on the what ifs Take a fear inventory. What are you worried or scared about in your professional life? Analyse, assess the risks, then let them go. Will you be fired if you take a two-week holiday, or if you can't make a meeting because your child is sick? Not if you're a valuable team member the rest of the time, and not if the company you work for is one that is worthy of you.

Consider if you're a candidate for work–life blending rather than work–life balancing. Blending the two together – where your social life, creative outlets and me time are intertwined with your profession – might be right for you if you truly love your work, your career is your hobby and you are always thirsty to know more about your chosen field. Don't push for a separation if you are happy with it all melding together and you love the people in your industry. As a writer, my greatest happiness comes from conversations with other authors and journalists, attending my book club, hiking while listening to a memoir on Audible, or going to the cinema or theatre to study the art of storytelling. I try to pull my friends and family with different paths into my arena, too. My life is all a bit words heavy ... and I wouldn't want it any other way. You might feel the same; just check that other aspects of your personality are not being neglected.

Journal your journey – work

When your work life is feeling overwhelming, or dull, rip out a page of your work agenda and note down five things that you love about your role. It could be your colleagues, the pay cheque, the office with a fabulous cappuccino machine, the sense of identity working for the company gives you, or getting away from your role of partner and parent for a few hours a day. If you're having a particularly bad day, or patch, write down five jobs you've had in the past that have been even worse – or bosses who have been even worse. Any of these exercises will help you to get some perspective.

Cutting out colleagues

If you're like me, a team player who generally expects the best from people, it can be shocking to find yourself in a work situation where people would sell their own granny – and certainly sell you out – to get in with a boss. Colleagues can be a great resource for comfort during trying times, long hours, brain-storms and manager upheavals, but, if possible, you need to remember that you're all looking out for yourselves. Keep com-plaints, gossip and personal fears out of the office and within close non-work friends' groups and family. Too often informa-tion you've shared in confidence with a colleague who is on your side gets into the wrong hands, or just becomes the subject of office chit-chat, which can be hurtful, professionally unhelpful and a waste of your time to correct or clear up. Don't share any-thing you wouldn't want to get back to your boss or HR.

Don't get too drunk at office parties and don't do anything you wouldn't want your mum to see. A woman I worked with once did a knickerless cartwheel at a Christmas work gathering and for the rest of her time in the job, despite her wonderful work, she was known as 'Fur Coat No Knickers Fiona' because of her saucy gymnastics display. Don't be your company's flash-ing acrobat.

Confessions of a people-pleaser

Who can forget that sinking feeling you get when you find out, through social media or a 'well-meaning' friend, that you've been excluded from an important meeting, rejected for a promo-tion, not selected to go to the company's think-tank spa day, or turned down for a grant or endowment you worked hard to get? It sparks a horrible mix of FOMO and self-doubt. I've witnessed, over the years, desperate attempts by colleagues and friends to ingratiate themselves into certain company cultures, in-crowds in an office, societies or groups, using everything from their bank accounts (buying OTT gifts for their hard-to-win-over bosses) to plastic surgery and extreme dieting (believing that they have to look a certain way to fit into a certain work environment or to get ahead). Yes, in extreme cases, a deep-seated desire to be liked or valued can cause credit-card debt and extreme vanity – not just crippling self-doubt. In our social lives, popularity can make us feel happy and accepted – hugely important feelings – but in the workplace, popularity can be the key to getting a bonus, a promotion and living a day-to-day life free of dread, so how can we handle this pressure without losing our sense of self?

I know, all too well, the emotional distress that being unloved or being left out can bring in a professional sphere. Some people can shrug off not being liked. 'If they don't like me, their loss,' they say, before moving on, healthily, to concentrate on people who matter. But I've had to battle to become one of those self-assured individuals. I was already insecure due to the biological father who didn't love me, and that was made worse by a decade of being one of the uncool kids at school. Choosing to enter the media industry was a challenge: it was like heading into a boxing ring where egos and bylines are wrestled to the floor and held down until someone shouts 'I give up.' Despite having always had wonderful, close friends and a supportive family, professional brush-offs or failings were painful and personal, even when they shouldn't have been. My past made me take any kind of rejection painfully to heart – and it took me a while to realise that the problem was me, not colleagues who were too busy worrying about their own professional standing to care for my mental well-being. This deep-rooted need to be liked at the cost of my sanity or self-respect really hit home when I returned to university to do my masters. A professor took an instant dislike to me and her obvious disdain gave me insomnia, and my ankles flared up with hives. Instead of working with her, and her with me, to build a good understanding of university teachings and writing a dissertation, I nearly fell apart.

How I learnt to reset my rejection receptors

Let me take you back to a particularly awful three-hour class; a situation I fear many of you will have been in during meetings, at conferences, or – even worse – job interviews. Tears stung my eyes and my face burnt red-hot with humiliation and fear. *Don't cry, don't cry*, I urged myself, as my tormentor mocked me in front of 14 students gathered in the classroom, 'I mean what a stupid thing to say!' She glared at me disdainfully. I tugged at my ponytail until my hair fell loose around my shoulders, shielding my crumpled expression from their gaze. What had I done to make this woman hate me? I tried to be polite, professional, likeable. A lone, hot tear slid down my cheek. I wasn't a child. I was 37 years old. The reason I knew her dislike had nothing to do with the real me was because I saw the first flicker of hatred on the first day of term, as we went around the room introducing ourselves. At the end of the class, the 20-something I'd sat next to asked what our problem was. 'She hates you!' he said. 'What's your history? Have you taken a class together before?' I faked a carefree laugh and said I'd never met her before and that perhaps she didn't like blondes, or mature students, or Essex accents. 'Well, whatever it is, she is a scary lady. Rather you than me.' As the term went on, it got worse. I was miserable. In the days leading up to her class, I couldn't sleep. In the days following it, I'd have nightmares. I was so unsure of myself that I stopped enjoying my work – not just in her class but all my classes. I knew that however hard I worked, however punctual or decent I was, she would never treat me professionally or fairly. Have you been there with someone you have to deal with at work or university, a senior who has power over you? The mysterious unfairness of it all was what really dragged me down.

For someone who had always been a people-pleaser – not because I was naturally gregarious and fun, but because, even as a successful adult, I was petrified of feeling the hurt, sadness and loneliness I'd felt as a child – I found her dislike of me impossible to cope with healthily. Realising this and wanting to break these patterns, I went to talk to a therapist. 'The problem is hers, not yours,' he said when I told him I was always courteous, punctual and keen. 'You must be triggering something in her, perhaps you remind her of the woman her husband left her for, or the person who got the promotion she wanted, or someone who bullied her once. Regardless, if you are determined to finish your masters – and you should, this is your dream – go in there with your head held high, with sympathy for her.' He made me appreciate that her behaviour was not about me – neither was all the similar behaviour I had experienced in my life from bosses or colleagues who had left me feeling insecure in the past. He explained that I could train myself not to care so much about others' opinions of me. 'Her bullying says more about her than you.'

He taught me a couple of tricks to rewire my rejection receptors: a visualisation of moments when I felt strong and successful, and breathing techniques to keep me calm (in for four through my nose, hold for four, out for eight through my mouth) and he promised he would be there for a pep talk whenever I needed one. He also urged me to spend time talking to people who were there for me and who I knew wanted the best for me. He reminded me that what happened in the classroom did not sum up my entire life. This is what I want you to take into difficult professional situations, too. Your professional life is not the sum of your parts: you have family and friends, hobbies and interests, self-care and alone time that is invaluable. You are not defined by how other people value your worth.

The professor was as vile to me as usual that first day post-therapy, but I remembered to breathe steadily, and to remember times in my life when I'd felt confident: when I'd got my A level results, when I'd gone swimming with sharks, when I'd managed a difficult meeting successfully. The ruder she got, the more I smiled and thanked her for her input. She looked shell-shocked. Her face was a picture. At first this was mock bravado. Inside, I was still scared, waiting for the next assault. But after a month my pretend confidence became second nature and I approached each lesson like a gladiator going into battle, calling out her behaviour before it could hurt me. 'Now, I know you won't like my idea obviously, Professor, but ...' was a favourite phrase that would put her on the back foot – I'd already publicly acknowledged she wouldn't like it, I foresaw and owned her insults before she did, so what could she add? Picking on me must have been boring once my very visible reactions – tears, deep blushes and shaking hands – had subsided.

We actually ended our scholarly relationship on a cordial note when, despite telling me in our final meeting in front of everyone that the title of my thesis was the 'worst I've seen in all my years of teaching' a level of professionalism must have kicked in because she gave me the second highest grade in the class. I felt vindicated and proud of myself for working hard against my default position of thinking rejection must be my fault, keeping calm and carrying on. I'd revised my reaction to hurtful comments, edited out my need to please, and come out victorious.

I feel like I got my masters in literature *and* in people studies. I learnt to worry only about people who are worth worrying about. You really can't make everyone like you, even bosses who hired you or professors who accepted you on to their programme, however decently you behave, so just act in a way where you can like yourself. I still have this deep-seated desire to be part of the gang, which I may never shake. But I have now learnt when enough is enough – to not keep taking someone's rejection to heart, to let them go. I am still a people-pleaser who wants to be liked, but I've become more discerning today about who I want to please and who I need to be liked by, and at the top of that list is me.

How to keep calm and carry on without crying

Try these visualisation techniques to help you control your focus, quieten negative voices – both interior and exterior – and rebalance your emotions to a neutral or stronger state.

* Repeat a mantra, a thought or a feeling until it becomes second nature. Choose a time when you felt powerful and in control. Whenever you feel yourself spinning away from sanity, close your eyes, travel back

to this place, and allow your heart to be bolstered by the knowledge that you *can* do it, you can *be* it.

- If something tricky or challenging is approaching, think forward and put yourself in the situation. Visualise it all going well, with you feeling smart and your answers making sense, knowing it doesn't have to be perfect, just good. Rehearse, rehearse, rehearse!

- Think of someone you know who always sounds and looks confident, in control and knowledgeable, not arrogant or smug. Take on their characteristics. Mimic their stance, their greeting, their walk. Try on their persona for size, see how it feels and adapt the best bits to suit you.

Getting real: Samantha, 30

'As I've got older and busier (or perhaps wiser, but probably just busier) what with the kids *and* work *and* running the home and doing all that general adulting stuff, I've been forced to say no to more things, and become more realistic about what I can get done while keeping my sanity in check. I know I could make everyone beautiful handmade gifts, bake everything from scratch, attend every meeting and decorate the house to within an inch of its life, but the truth is I can't do all that and remain a reasonable human being. When I've taken on too much in the past, or said yes to too many things, I've inevitably got everything done (because that's how I operate when I have a "to do" list), but I often then feel overwhelmed and exhausted, and the people who pay the price are those nearest and dearest to me who wonder why I'm suddenly deafening them with yells about not putting a dirty plate in the dishwasher. And it's that feeling of being overwhelmed that holds a magnifying glass over every normally inconsequential hiccup, making everything feel stressful, strained and joyless. I've learnt to say no to more, and take on less, at work and at home. And I don't feel guilty, because I know I am a better, more rational, reasonable colleague, partner and parent for it.'

Teamwork makes the dream work

Being a boss is difficult; being an underling is difficult. You have to manage down and up (and up, in my experience, is always the most challenging). It's easy to get very, very attached to a team who you have hired, championed and seen grow in a really great way. In my first annual evaluation when I was the editor-in-chief of *OK!* my boss declared my only negative mark was that I defended my employees 'like a mother lioness, reasonable judgement out the window'. I'm a stereotypical Leo, loyal and proud, so I've always known that I veer in this direction, but I had to rein it in a little when I became the boss of 50 people – some of whom were great, some of whom needed to be pushed to be greater and some of whom needed a firmer hand and discipline. I had to learn to be a manager, and when I did it made the whole team stronger. Building a content crew, from within it, or when you're in charge of it, isn't easy – but here's some useful advice:

Cut the BS A problem shared is a problem halved. If you can, without disclosing private and confidential information you are forbidden to from up above, be honest with your cohort about timelines, goals and the needs and issues that need sorting. Keep your team informed and they'll stay more engaged. They will enjoy being in your trusted inner circle, and feel part of the solution. Praise regularly, and never take credit for anyone else's ideas or labour. That's just shit, and the opposite of authentic.

Don't sit in the shadows keeping your opinions to yourself. Raise questions thoughtfully and politely, interrupt biased remarks or negative chatter calmly but firmly, educate and encourage your team to seek positive goals, and echo team members who speak truth to power, make sense, and have good ideas. We underestimate the power of adding one voice to another's, but those two voices can bring great changes and make great waves.

Learn to listen This is harder than we sometimes think, but active listening can help companies to grow, diversify and prosper. Listen to your head and heart, and then listen to viewpoints offered from those around you. Don't be so set in your ways and methods that you refuse to see a benefit in what someone else is saying. Don't interrupt. Listen, and ask for more information. Run the team as democratically as makes sense.

Show authentic commitment to your comrades and your projects. Contribute, compliment and show up when it matters. Be flexible, get done what needs to be done, and don't dial it in. If your mental bandwidth is a bit low at some points, explain, if you can, and still do what is expected of you, just politely refuse the extras – and thank those that are more than pulling their weight for you en masse. Be reliable and responsible. Don't get known as the flake who lets the team down.

Be a helper: become someone who others can turn to for support. Be a problem-solver: become a safe space for debate. Be an apologiser: become a colleague who isn't afraid to admit that they were wrong and move on.

Getting real: Helen, 32

'A powerful problem which affects my mental well-being is untidiness, so I make time every day to ensure that I arrive to an ordered and tidy desk at work, and return to an ordered and tidy house each evening. If my surroundings are a mess – piles of paperwork, pens that don't work, unpaid invoices, kids' and husband's clothes everywhere, messy dog prints, dishes left out – I can literally feel my head throbbing with anxiety. As soon as everything is clear and tidy, I feel my mood lift – it's so strange how the two are interlinked. I know myself well enough to know that just a five-minute sweep of debris at work and home straightens my mind. I take charge; I am in charge.'

Own your story – here's how

It's time to check in and note, score and plan your most authentic, happy work life going forward.

*A*ct immediately

Small is beautiful. You can implement healthy, tiny edits today – commit to being home by 6pm for family dinners at least three times a week, start taking healthy snacks in with you to work rather than lurking round the sugar-dosing chocolate machines, show gratitude to your colleagues who've helped you out, which will boost their mood and yours.

*U*rgent and important, say yes

If it's not urgent or important, say no – that's how you need to prioritise your free time outside the office, thereby safeguarding your chances to relax away from work.

*T*rack your day

Work in a way that suits your personality. If you're a morning person, push through the hard stuff straight away, but book meetings and brainstorms for after lunch when you're moving a bit slower. Night owl? Plan for the day ahead or undertake research in the silence when everyone else is asleep.

*H*ave realistic expectations

What can you achieve in a day or a week? You can't please all the people all the time without losing your ▶

mind. Do a little self-analysis: what is working for you and the team? How can issues be fixed? Can anything be delegated? Is anything a waste of time?

$\mathcal{E}$ xpand your strengths

Don't try to be everything to everyone, focus on what you're good at and what comes easily, or what you have a natural interest in. If you're weak in an area you need, don't be shy in asking for training or looking into an online course.

$\mathcal{N}$ arrow down negative influences

Is someone making you doubt yourself? Do they know what they're talking about, or are they playing some kind of wicked game? Don't listen to anything without first understanding (a) why they're sharing this information; (b) if they have your best interests at heart; and (c) getting to grips with office politics and deciphering the good from the bad.

$\mathcal{T}$ ake time to find a mentor

You can learn a lot from people who have been there and done that in your area, you can also gain a lot from becoming a mentor to someone starting out (updated perspectives, insight into a new demographic, and so on). Nurture your network. If no one stands out, consider hiring a business coach who can help you get rid of self-harming habits and build better ones.

$\mathcal{I}$ dentify the time wasters

Draw up boundaries so that your quality time – professionally and personally – is devoted to people and pursuits high up on your love scale. Allow someone to take you for a ride once but never again. Learn who feeds your career, and who sucks it dry.

C hange your work–life structure to suit you

If you don't ask, you don't get – so ask for a different work schedule if it will suit you and your family, ask to work from home a couple of days a week, ask to buy extra holiday days, tell colleagues that you are not replying to demands at weekends unless catastrophe awaits. If you want to try freelance work, do the maths and think logistically about how it can work. If you're working from home and hate it, ask your network how office culture has changed – you might want to go back – and if they hear of any openings, to let you know. Don't rose-tint any scenario. There are pluses and minuses to all working situations; you just need to work through what is right for you. Be the change you need.

Chapter 8

All You Need is Love

'Love takes off masks that we fear we cannot live without
and know we cannot live within.'

James Baldwin

True love is the key to a happy life. An authentic love of self, a universal love for something bigger than ourselves, familial love, romantic love, love for friends and community. Love does not come in a one-size-fits-all format; and love is not a static expression of joy ... but there is nothing more worth fighting for. And sometimes it will feel like a fight. Because love is a many-splendoured thing, and it can lift us up. But never be in doubt that love is also a battlefield. Love can also be blind. There is no greater time when we need to know our real desires, goals and joys than in affairs of the heart. It is in our deepest interactions with other human beings that we can feel at our happiest and most able to be authentic, assured that we can be treasured, warts and all. What a shame that pesky things like lust, pride, greed and insecurity get in the way so often.

Wouldn't it be marvellous if we could love and be loved in return purely for what we are? Too often, we find ourselves so wound up in desire, or in a drive for perfection, or dazzled by a shiny new suitor, that we let people down that we should cherish, or we allow legit affection to slip away, or we serve up a steaming plate of trouble that starves us of meaningful connections.

Love, oh love! What lessons we have to learn. When it comes to my family and friends, I hope I have never missed a chance to show them that I love them, that I'm thinking of them and working out ways to spend quality time with them. But when it has come to my romantic relationships, it has taken me far longer to shake Eros by the hand and be able to look him in the eye. If we're honest, we all have moments when we are hard to love, ask too much, give too little and act too harshly. And we all have moments when, sunk under heavy, lonely bones or crying in nightclub toilets, we beg for someone to truly see us and to love us with all they have. And we've all had moments when we have focused our attention on the wrong person, someone who doesn't see us in our genuine glory, someone who moulds us to their will or dismisses us as lesser. Yes, love is a losing game too often. But when we connect – be it with a friend, our own child, or a new lover – nothing is more beautiful.

Lessons in love

There are no rules, but you can give yourself the best shot at finding your equal when you know yourself and know what makes you happy:

Before you open yourself up to love, reflect honestly on your part in the failure of past relationships. It would be easier to place 100 per cent of the blame for your misery on the other person, but consider whether you were happy in yourself? You need to acknowledge your part in past failings and start loving yourself, or expect the same conclusions at your next attempt to partner up.

Drop the games and masks Flirting and playing is fun when you're not looking for anything serious, but when you are, admit it to yourself and your romantic interest. Express yourself without ambiguity.

Keep an eye out for emotional manipulation A partner shouldn't make you second-guess yourself, shouldn't make you feel trapped and shouldn't be too needy. They should want you to flourish. The path of true love never did run smooth, but be aware when issues become deeper than quirks, niggles and getting used to each other. Don't give someone total power over you, your appearance, your social circle or your bank balance. A worthy suitor wouldn't want to take control of these things.

Communicate – frequently, calmly and without over-expressing or exaggeration. Check how you talk to others – and yourself. When you have a healthy inner dialogue, you'll find it easier to lead healthier conversations in a relationship.

Be selfish, and allow your partner to be selfish. Encourage each other to keep your friends, your hobbies, your alone time, your routine. When they deserve to enter these aspects of your life, they will do so naturally and effortlessly, and it will feel good. Cling on to what makes you happy. Don't give over your true self to someone else. The resentment will fester; your authentic self buried until it suffocates.

Never settle Don't think of yourself as running out of time, or not good enough, or bow to every whim of someone who does not deserve you. You are good enough – you are more than enough. Healthy relationships are built on mutual respect and admiration.

Finish unfinished business It isn't fair to pull someone into a love triangle that they know nothing about.

The lament of the unloved

The most passionate moment of my life happened when I kissed a boy I thought I loved on the escalator at Holborn Underground station. As he bent down to touch my lips with his, I got an electric shock. A full-on power surge. 'Please tell me you felt that?' I said, my legs buckling as we whizzed up to daylight, past posters for West End shows and Capital FM. He nodded his breathtaking smile, and kissed me again. This was it then, I thought. You can't get a physical, visceral buzz through your entire body when you kiss someone and not want to be with them for ever. I was 21 and naïve about many things around relationships, and I was willing to hand him my heart on a platter. I'd loved him for two years at this point, since the moment I first spotted him across the sticky floor of a pub while I was at university. We'd never officially dated. I wasn't introduced to his family, or welcomed into his social circle, and once at a party – in a moment that made me retch in the street as friends rubbed my back – he'd shamelessly snogged a polished, posh girl, who made me feel like common rubbish, easily discardable, in front of me. But I kept returning to him, convinced he would want me one day, as I wanted him every day. That he'd see my value and how I would be there for him, loyal and loving.

I tried to change who I was for him, to heighten aspects that I thought he'd like and to quash traits I thought he wouldn't. I put on a haughty accent and dressed how the other private-school girls did, started watching rugby and hanging around his part of the city. None of it worked. Even though physically, we sparked, he wouldn't take me for his. *But at last! This will change everything*, I imagined seconds after our voltaic embrace. It didn't. We made our way out into the hustle, hand in hand, and spent one more night together, then I didn't see him again. He got back with an ex – his first love, the one *his* entire body sparked for – and I was left heartbroken, bereft and vulnerable to the next person who could snap me up on the rebound.

Hit it, then quit it

The tragic truth about affairs of the heart is that you can't make someone love you. You can't tap them on the shoulder and recite a list of all your positive qualities; you can't sell yourself to someone who doesn't want to buy. The timing might be wrong, they might already be in love with someone else, you could be ringing alarm bells that are not of your doing but coming from their past or their insecurities. You can give it your all; you owe it to yourself to fight for love – but you also need to know when enough is enough. Send an authentic message to your beloved: share your feelings, your wishes, but when you get nothing in return (just unfaithfulness, abuse, coldness or disinterest), do leave it well alone. If they see the light, and they are courageous enough to accept what is authentically best for them, they will return to you and win you back – if you let them. But while you're begging, being too needy or altering your personality in a bid to be alluring, they will not get a chance to realise how wonderful the *real* you is. And the *real* you is the only one you can live with in the long term.

Falling in love is easy; falling out of love is very hard. Edit the heartbreak from your life at your own pace, learning to love yourself truly before looking for anyone else. Heal your heart by:

Allowing yourself to feel the pain Don't numb or shut off the grief with alcohol, drugs or denial. That would be inauthentic and all the dormant, unworked-through feelings will explode at some point (mine did, hence my difficult first marriage). Spend time with yourself, working out your part in the upset, if there are any lessons you can learn from it, about yourself and how you are in a partnership. Cry, too, if you want to – unabashedly. Tears contain toxic biochemical by-products, and a hearty weep clears them out and relieves emotional stress.

Enjoying your freedom by picking up things that you've neglected during your stressful relationship days; the things you'd given up to try to please your partner, or replaced with pastimes you didn't really love to impress them. No more watching shows or going places because you think it will earn you brownie points. Do only the things that make you happy – the real you as a separate entity from them. Pick up your friendships, hobbies and relaxation techniques. Promise never to abandon your true self to a love affair again, and certainly commit to not neglecting your other relationships when you do fall in love again. Forgive well-meaning friends who try to fix you up with someone before you're ready, or who tell you they never liked your ex anyway. They are not perfect heart-menders, they are just trying to help in their own way.

Focusing on your well-being Getting enough sleep (to limit mood swings and irritability) and eating healthily (omega-3s, vitamin B12 and folic acid are natural antidepressants) are invaluable. Exercise increases serotonin and norepinephrine, both physiological boosters, allowing you to take control and feel positive. Dancing has a therapeutic effect, so blast the radio or your favourite childhood pop songs and move.

Reclaiming your future When you feel yourself sliding into a pile of self-loathing, pick up a pen and write down your qualities. Be honest about your low self-esteem with friends and family, and ask them to share positive thoughts and messages, too. Write a bucket list: short- and long-term things that you want to do that will make you happy. Mostly, be kind to yourself. Yes, your life hasn't turned out the way you wanted it to, but your life still deserves to be magnificent. Imagine yourself a year on from your heartbreak. You will feel better.

Unfollowing them from your world, online and IRL. You don't need to see your ex-partner's new partner on social media, so block them. You don't need to see their toothbrush every morning, so throw it away. You don't need to risk bumping into them at a restaurant they introduced you to, so rethink your routes. Limit your emotional collateral by rebuilding a world focused on you and your peace of mind. This is not running away. This is not weakness. This is safeguarding your mental health.

Escaping your own woes and helping other people. Most of us are going through something, whether we show it or not. Connect with people on a meaningful level, volunteer, engage in your community. As a collective whole, everyone will be boosted by caring, sharing and gratitude – and being honest about what struggles we face. Don't feel ashamed of having a broken heart. Your vulnerability will allow other people to address their unfinished feelings. Do show caution on social media, however, and remember that everything you share can be saved by others, and you never truly know your audience. Besides, a hug or a hand held is much more reassuring than a blinking computer screen.

Forgiving them (and yourself if you played a part) ... and daring to find love again. Let go of your anger, gain perspective on what happened and the lies you were telling yourself, and give the love you were saving for them to people who deserve it – your pets, your family, your colleagues, until you find a partner again. Because you will. Statistically, you must trust that you will love again. Even those whose hearts have been hung, drawn and quartered by a partner's death, find love again. Meeting a new partner does not discount what you felt before, it just proves that you are strong, worthy of love and that you are human.

Back to my broken heart

Eventually, ten years after I swooned on that Holborn escalator, and now with a rebound marriage and divorce under my belt, my ex-lover and I met up in Covent Garden. He, too, had just got divorced – from the woman he'd loved too much to ever consider my devotion seriously. We reminisced for hours, we snuck a kiss in drizzly lamplight, and I walked away pleased that I finally had the closure I needed to move on. You see, I'd rose-tinted him for a decade, always thinking of his handsome face and what could have been. That night I was faced with the real him, not my imagined version of him. The ten years that had passed allowed me to treat him as an equal rather than fawning over him and placing him on a pedestal (running a successful magazine in New York will do that to a girl). He was employed by his dad because he didn't like 'working hard', he was bald with a beer belly, and he still chain-smoked, a trait everyone else I knew had given up soon after leaving behind the exam-cramming, essay-writing heady days of university. He'd never learnt to drive, because his friends were used to being his chauffeur. And the worst, after we'd kissed in the rain on Floral Street, and my heart skipped a dangerous beat, he made a confession. He was engaged, he was getting married again in a few months, but a kiss with me didn't count as being unfaithful, because it was for old times' sake, and by the same logic, a quickie back at his wouldn't either. I assured him it did, and, as if by magic, this mythical creature I'd put my love life on hold for was revealed to me.

As I travelled back to New York the following day, I realised what a blessing our meeting had been. My heart was no longer frozen by this disappointing Adonis; he was no longer my Achilles heel. The rose-tinted glasses were off for good, crushed under my stiletto heel. There were no more 'what ifs'. I was able to move forward, no longer making comparisons to this ghost of my boyfriend past. And that is a great place to be mentally when you're about to meet your forever lover. Or should I say, re-meet.

Love stories

Ten must-reads for an honest portrait of relationships:

- *Three Women* by Lisa Taddeo
- *An American Marriage* by Tayari Jones
- *On Chesil Beach* by Ian McEwan
- *Olive Kitteridge* by Elizabeth Strout
- *The Colour Purple* by Alice Walker
- *The Beggar Maid* by Alice Munro
- *Giovanni's Room* by James Baldwin
- *To the Lighthouse* by Virginia Woolf
- *Mating in Captivity* by Esther Perel
- *Things My Mother Never Told Me* by Blake Morrison

Trusting my gut, twice: a love story

I have always been a list-maker. I have, since I was a teen, written thought-out, no-nonsense records of what I had to achieve that day (taking geeky glee in crossing things off), or I have divided a sheet of paper into a tally of pros and cons to help me solve a difficult dilemma. Lists, it seemed, cleared the way of mental debris to a point of succinct and clear purpose. Clutter removed, resolutions could be weighed and acted upon. I could write columns of things to say yes or no to; people who I could trust or couldn't. Lists were perfect editing tools to make me happy.

In 2008, a few years after my divorce, an ill-fated love affair that lasted too long, and a spell of singledom, I met a life coach who had a reputation as being a bit of a love guru. I told him that finally I was ready to meet someone, but that I couldn't think where to start. I was living in New York at the time, holding down the job that kept me in the office 12 hours a day, and the American dating scene left me confused. The love guru told me that I could conjure up Mr Right easily, that it was all about three things: positive thinking, working out what I really wanted and willpower. He told me about one trick that never failed, in all aspects of life: 'Write a list of what you genuinely want, pin it somewhere where you will see it every day, read it, will it, imagine the list coming true.' It sounded too easy. 'Write down 20 things you want in a man. Do it today.' Twenty? I went home and tried to do as he said, but twenty? I was desperate by the end – adding things like 'must support Tottenham Hotspur FC', 'have blue eyes' which are clearly daft and unnecessary when looking for a life partner. But buoyed by the love guru's positivity, I pinned the list to my fridge and looked at it each morning and night, accepting that even if it didn't work, per se, at least it was making me edit out what I *didn't* want, which had tripped me up in past relationships, falling for men who clearly weren't right for me.

Two months later, out of the blue, an ex-boyfriend from university emailed me. He'd bumped into a mutual friend at a party in London, discussed me fondly, and got my email. He'd always wondered how I was and where I was. He, randomly, was living in America too, so he thought he'd get in touch. He'd never been married. He was currently single. He was everything on my list, even a blue-eyed Spurs fan. Six weeks later he proposed; six months later we were married. The list had worked! 'I told you!' my love guru sent me a message on my wedding day. 'With clear ideas of what you should say yes and no to, you can be happy.'

I was smug in my happy-ever-after zone – and then the seven-year itch hit our marriage. Well, young children hit, and perhaps the dulling of the initial rush of lust and endorphins that a deep love affair sets sail with. Instead of appreciating what I'd found when I thought back to the list I'd written all those years ago, I cursed myself for not writing things like 'must love building Lego' and 'enjoys getting up very early, even at weekends, to change nappies'. We were on rocky waters. Not in our love and respect for each other, which was still there, but in connecting on a daily basis and being kind to one another. Living away from family we would go months at a time without going on a date, our intimacy faded, and we lost the reasons we'd fallen in love with each other under the grind. We were still a team, but domesticity had pushed out desirability.

Everyone in a long-term relationship knows how hard it is to keep even the smallest spark of passion alive when you're too exhausted to maintain the sex life you once had, or when the character traits you found so charming at the start of your romance begin to irritate, or when insomniac toddlers and work worries take over. My husband, Russell, and I had drifted, quite unknowingly, from being love's young dream to a stressed middle-aged couple who discussed mortgage payments as we flossed our teeth each night, before sinking appreciatively into our pillows to stare at our phones without so much as a kiss goodnight. We no longer talked lovingly about the future, just barked instructions in each other's general direction. Was this just a phase we were experiencing, or the beginning of the end? Either way, I knew our marriage needed a close read of the things we were both doing wrong – and right – and a good, ruthless edit. I was not prepared for us to sink, and remembering how writing a list had worked so powerfully for me in finding Russell, I put pen to paper once again.

A list for my lover

I jotted down all the things I loved about him, including detailed things such as 'he shares cooking responsibilities', 'he is kind to my friends and helps them out whenever I ask him', and 'he fills my car up with petrol because he knows it's a chore I hate' and put the paper in my bedside drawer. It was not the most romantic list, but it was full of concrete reasons why he made my life better. My first list was all the things I hoped to find in a partner – a wish list embodied by Russ – and the second list was actually about who he was and how he legitimately made my life better. When, two weeks later, I felt a pre-menstrual fury rise in my chest when he said something unintentionally thoughtless, instead of flying off the handle as I usually did, my eyes rolling around in their sockets like a bag of marbles in a disco-dancer's pocket, I took some time out. I picked one thing from the list, reminisced on an example, took a deep breath and remembered that although we were in the thick of child-raising and that work could be stressful, I was right to pick Russ. My docket became a material marriage counsellor of sorts, a mode of self-therapy. The first list had helped me to find him, and the second helped me to value him. I could have written a tally of all the things I wanted to change about him, or regretted not having, but I went for positivity and focused on all the good things we already had and how lucky we were. He noticed a change immediately, so I told him about my secret list and offered to let him read it. He was underwhelmed by the practical, unromantic reasons that had prompted this attitude of gratitude but thankful that I wasn't quite so snappy and picky. I became kinder; he became kinder.

This was five years ago and our marriage has been restored, mostly. My marital edit with a twist worked – and it reminded me of the power of writing down what is important, saying yes to joy and positivity, and staying focused on the overwhelming good core of a person rather than the merely irritating, which can be hard to do in the red-mist moments of relationships, and not comparing your partnership to those you see around you. It really reminded me, and still does, as I revisit the list to add things to it every so often, how important it is not to take love – or a person – for granted, even when you have a legal contract. Our relationships need to be frequently, judiciously and honestly edited to ensure that we are focused on not only where we are, but also on where we want to go ... together. Without careful editing, relationships can go stale and get lost.

Getting real: Geri, 41

'After my painful divorce, I've worked out that relationships need to be less like Beyoncé's "Crazy in Love" and more The Beatles' "When I'm 64". I am more mature and I understand that partnerships are about hard work, setting boundaries and limits, and protecting that relationship from external time and energy zappers. For me, post-divorce relationships feel more considered. Going through a divorce means going through a huge, public life edit, and when it happened to me, I felt exposed, raw and vulnerable ... but I had this wealth of information and experience in the bag. I was stripped down to my most authentic self, and although I had days – no, weeks – when I felt like an empty shell, I also knew that if I survived it, I could survive anything. I feel that the next time I head into a serious relationship I'll be able to be more honest with myself and my partner, and have the self-esteem to walk away when things aren't working, knowing I'll survive because I have before.'

Journal your journey – your relationship

Sit down with your partner, a pen and some paper. Make a note of three new rules – small, big or seemingly silly as you desire, it doesn't matter – you just have to agree on them. It will give you the chance to revisit your relationship priorities. Do you put away your phones while you're eating dinner? If not, perhaps write that? Do you still kiss each other when you get back from work? If not, perhaps add that. Find three things you both agree on that would help maintain connection and affection during trying, boring times.

Meet the parents

Meeting your beloved's parents for the first time is always nerve-wracking and you might be tempted to put on a bit of a show and pretend to be something you're not. It never works. Mothers are too smart for these shenanigans (I feel sorry for whoever my poor children bring home; I already have my interrogation lamp waiting in the loft). Being a divorcée makes meeting the parents even more awkward. Although second marriage after a divorce is common in the UK, a second-time bride carries a stigma.

I remember meeting my second set of future in-laws for the first time. On top of the usual nerves, I was petrified about the judgement I might receive. My partner's parents knew only a handful of things about me, one of which was that I'd been divorced four years earlier, after a marriage in my early twenties. At 34 years old, I felt like an imposter as I walked red-cheeked into a Hertfordshire pub to meet my future mother and father-in-law (who, incidentally, had been childhood sweethearts and had been married for decades). Would they think that I was second-hand goods, ensnaring their innocent son (who hadn't even lived with a girlfriend) into a trap? Or did they presume that I was just no good at commitment or that I was hiding some dark secrets about my past?

Desperate to address the elephant in the room, I decided to be real and confront my insecurities head-on with Russell's mother and sister the second time we met. 'Ask me anything you want,' I said, telling them no subject was off limits. I meant it. I wanted to build our new family from a place of honesty and authenticity. They stared at me wide-eyed as I summed up five years of drama about my previous relationship, including how opening my decree nisi and seeing a thick rubber stamp invalidating the hopes I once held so dear made me cry for three hours straight. Finally, I told them that having gone through the whole rigmarole of a big wedding before, like most second-time brides, I was now more focused on the marriage and the man than the trappings of the day. I remember his mother taking my hand in hers. 'We're just happy Russell is happy.' She smiled. I was overwhelmed with a raw, honest emotion. We need to remember that this is the crux of it all: families just want their loved ones to be happy. Delete made-up dramas and doubts from your interactions.

Editing yourself a happy ending – for real, this time!

Only someone who has had their heart dragged through a wringer after a difficult cohabitation, or a divorce court, can truly appreciate the hours of self-reflection that will come with getting yourself ready for a second attempt at living with someone or a second marriage. They know that delving into the psychology of relationships brings many positives to the next attempt, which far outweigh the social stigma and sniggers of observers, or your own sense of being a failure. Experience makes us more confident that we're making an informed decision this time. I can tell you that when you make a public mistake like marrying the wrong person in front of everyone you love and respect, you'll do everything in your power to make sure it never happens again. You know what you want from a husband and, more importantly, you know what you don't want, and you can feel confident that you're making an informed decision. I entered my second marriage knowing that I never wanted to leave it, that I'd use everything in my arsenal: honesty, realism and (if necessary) couples therapy.

I wasn't expecting a fairy-tale the second time around. To marry again, to reveal your feelings to the world again after the failure and heartbreak of a divorce means that you really do believe in love; you're stripped down and vulnerable in your desire to build a relationship that makes you happy. Making a mess of it the first time only made me more determined to find the right partner and give marriage a second chance. What's more, I think I understood better what marriage meant: hard work, democracy, mediation. 'The biggest benefit of marrying for a second time is the self-awareness that it brings,' explained my friend, couples therapist Katherine Loyd, who knows from her professional and personal experience that using what you learnt, or didn't learn, from your first marriage can only be positive in your second. 'There's a truth pill we're forced to swallow when we get divorced and remarry. We are making the decision to love and trust again, choosing to appreciate the reality of being in a relationship, rather than pushing for things to be exactly the way we want them to be, as we may have done naively the first time. In choosing to acknowledge what is actually available to us, we release ourselves from dwelling on fantasies of what should be, and see life as it really is.'

Getting real: Hannah, 35

'I remarried six months ago, after careful contemplation about what to change about my own behaviour. There was deep self-analysis after my first marriage broke down – a thorough edit of my expectations. I realised that I'd chosen my ex based on who I thought I ought to marry, who could give me what I wanted at that time. Going into my second marriage, I considered in much more depth whether we worked well as a team, with shared interests and ambitions that we both wanted to achieve together over the long term. My thoughts turned towards the authentic, not the trivial or frivolous.'

Focus on the long term

Authentic questions to ask yourself before embarking on a serious relationship:

- Have you given yourself enough time to really get to know the person you're about to commit to? And to get to know what you truly need?
- Could you be rushing into a decision because of a craving for security or social acceptance, or a fear of getting old or missing out on children?
- Do you know everything you need to know about your partner, and their friends and family? These other players will be in your life whether you've chosen them or not.

Band of gold

One advantage to getting married in your thirties – for the first or second time – is that by this age you really know who your friends are and who you want to watch you get hitched. I didn't feel pressured to invite distant relatives, parents' friends or colleagues because I knew – after the first one – that saying your vows (and hitting the dance floor) means more when you're surrounded by only your nearest and dearest. Some friends will have been to your previous wedding if you've had one, of course, but people go to so many these days so don't think that they're sitting there comparing the two. Still, do you need to edit your planning if it is your second wedding, or after living with a different partner for years, or having had children? The only thing I want you to edit is yourself – to a place of happiness and comfort. This is a day to celebrate love stories and next chapters. Face the future and any dilemmas you may feel head-on. Here are some common ones:

Should your parents shell out again if they paid for your previous wedding, or pay for your first when you're earning your own money? No, unless they make a genuine offer and it will make them happy. Only spend what you can afford and enjoy the freedom that brings. My parents intervened much more in my first wedding when they were helping me financially. Second time around, when my husband and I paid for everything, I didn't feel the need to curtail my desires to fit their ideals.

Gift lists? I felt cheeky asking for gifts at my second wedding, so we told everyone 'their presence was our present'. We were just grateful that they travelled from all over the world to be with us to celebrate. Many did still buy us gifts though. They felt I shouldn't be penalised for making a mistake in my past and that my husband certainly shouldn't be punished because this, after all, was his first wedding. Leave the decision up to your guests rather than thrusting material demands on them.

Can you wear white, even if you're a mum, or a divorcée? Who really has the right to wear a white gown when you look at what it is supposed to signify? Abandon ideas that you're not allowed to! All I cared about was making my groom happy, and I knew that he'd want me to wear a white dress. Any tut-tuts were just white noise.

When I walked down the aisle towards his massive smile, I knew that I'd made the right decision. My advice to other second-time brides who are being pushed towards a pastel suit or knee-length cream number is to stick up for themselves. Go for it! If that means you want a train, a veil and cascading bouquet, who cares?

Are bridesmaids acceptable at any age, at any type or size of wedding? Totally. What a great way to reward your best friends for being there throughout all the trials and tribulations of your love life in recent years. I had eight adult women support me up the aisle at my second wedding and felt so proud that they were there alongside me as I jumped into the future.

Should you include children from your previous relationships? Yes! This is a new beginning for you as a family, and you should start it as you mean to go on: making everyone feel special and included. I was a flower girl when my mother remarried and I remember being very proud and happy as I sat in the front row of the register office, clutching my posy and wearing a vintage velvet frock coat. I felt that I, too, was making a commitment to my stepfather to love him very much. My mum concurs. 'It only felt right to have my children standing up there with me. I wouldn't have got married again without your consent and contentment.'

Can you fire your family?

For me, the phrase 'blood is thicker than water' has never held much weight. I think we build our own families from relations *and* friends, editing our support network into a structure that makes us happy, and it's not dependent on shared DNA or obligation. Still, it's hard for people to cut out their family – it feels daring, angry and a bit shocking. It's always headline news isn't it, when a celebrity 'divorces' her manager parents, or when someone in the public eye refuses to engage with a parent who's suddenly crawled out of the woodwork when the lure of money and fame shrouds the child they once abandoned. It's even bigger news if a member of the royal family decides to step away from family traditions and form a new family system.

I feel less outrage than most. I feel their pain and imagine that they've had to take those steps to form a barrier of self-protection, because I too have cut off all contact with my birth father and his family, and I have never regretted it. I have only seen him once as an adult. I was 19 years old and shopping with a friend when I heard a voice I recognised behind me. As the hair on the back of my neck stood up, I knew it was him and turned around to see what his reaction would be. He carried on his conversation with the woman he was schmoozing, looked me up and down and turned back again with no flicker of recognition. I felt a wave of nausea and stumbled away before bursting into tears. My friend followed me in horror and couldn't understand my mad ramblings. Later, back home and calm, my overwhelming feeling was one of relief: he didn't know me. He had never been a major influence on my life.

This is why news I received in my thirties baffled me. An old friend of his, randomly bumping into my mother, told her that on his desk at work was a mini shrine to me. There were pictures and copies of my articles, and when visitors asked what it was all about he happily filled them in on his author daughter, who had inherited his height, good luck and way with words. When

I last saw him all those years ago, he didn't recognise me. But when I became a success, he started showing a public interest. What a shame that he didn't feel the same when I was a child desperately in need of her father's affection. Finding out about my errant father's pride unnerved me. I pushed him to the back of my mind when he pushed me aside, so, when this long-lost family acquaintance revealed his renewed interest in me, I felt scared that he'd try to find me and angry that he was taking credit. I was also confused – should I contact him, shouldn't I? Ultimately, I came to a conclusion that shocks people who haven't dealt with a toxic parent or sibling that picks and chooses their time to love them: blood is *not* thicker than water.

You do not owe a parent or sibling anything just because you share genetics. If you find love, support and honesty in friendships over family, well done! As someone who understands that not all familial love is constant and unconditional, I recommend that you edit out family who treat you badly, repeatedly.

How can you fill the holes this leaves?

- Set new boundaries for how you let people treat you. Look for the helpers. Search out people who understand you. Design a new village for your heart and head to happily reside in.
- Tell friends how special they are to you; treat them how you would a treasured family member. Be there for them so that they know they can rely on you. Invite them to share in your big moments. Communicate calmly and address conflict if it occurs – do not repeat familial bad habits with new, good people. Do not repeat toxic patterns.

- Give yourself time to reflect and heal, but remember that how they treated you is a reflection of them and their past and insecurities. You are nothing like them, and you are free.

In this world where we're running out of time and being pulled in a million directions, we should only make room for those who truly deserve the space. We don't need perfection from our family, but we do need consistency and love. That is why I happily reject the fake devotion of a father who doesn't deserve to be a part of my life, and I have fired him to protect my authentic self.

Own your story – here's how

It's time to check in and note, score and plan a life full of love; a life you deserve.

Acknowledge what you bring to a relationship
Don't go into a coupling thinking you're the lucky one, or you're lesser. The more you know your worth, the more apparent it becomes to others.

Use all your tricks
Make their life special; make your partnership special. As individuals and as a couple, provide tweaks and treats to boost your mood – special dates, alone time, little surprises. Your partner will feel cared for and your generosity will make you glow.

▶

$\mathcal{T}$ ake care of yourself

It doesn't matter if you're single, dating, or married, healthy habits and good hygiene are an aphrodisiac. Pay attention to how you feel, physically and mentally, whatever box you tick for relationship status. Love yourself first.

$\mathcal{H}$ ear your partner

Listen to your loved one so that they feel understood and accepted. When they feel heard, your intimacy and support for each other will be lifted, you'll feel connected and respected.

$\mathcal{E}$ xplore your body

Work out what makes you feel confident and sexy, how you enjoy physically expressing yourself. Swap shame for adventure. Make little life edits that make you feel sensual.

$\mathcal{N}$ arrow down biased influencers

When you're looking for love, don't immerse yourself in a group of singletons who hate romance and ridicule you for longing for it. When you're happily married, don't get in with a group of the bitchy betrothed, who are pushing for a group divorce response to their dire straits. Be a friend, listen, but safeguard your need for love from those who would crow, dissuade or ridicule you. Some people don't have your heart's best interests at heart, even if they are not aware of it.

$\mathcal{T}$ ake time to be alone

It is in silence, contemplation, meditation and daydreaming

that we can rejuvenate and truly relax. It is this version of you that will be most ready to face a new love, or to pursue a relationship, or to rebuild one that has got off track. Escape with yourself when needed. Don't give yourself completely to another.

$\mathcal{I}$ mperfections are a reality

Accept them. Everyone has their faults; you just need to work out if you can deal with your partner's. And when you realise that you *can* deal with them, you need to accept them, and even cherish them as part of their uniqueness. You can giggle at them, share them, ignore them – but know that no one is perfect.

$\mathcal{C}$ learly express your needs and desires

Speak up, ask for what you need, be confident that you are part of the conversation. Your partner will appreciate your forthrightness, as it makes their job easier. You can politely, calmly tell them what you want.

Chapter 9

The Optimism in Authenticity

'Keep trying, hold on, and always, always,
always believe in yourself, because if you don't, then
who will, sweetie? So, keep your head high, keep your
chin up, and most importantly, keep smiling, because life's
a beautiful thing and there's so much to smile about.'

Marilyn Monroe

The conveyor belt crowded with excess luggage we watch whizz by us every day is only going to get more cramped, crazy and dangerous as time marches on. For our own contentment, we need to forget about the suitcases of shame, lies, guilt and self-doubt that we carry around with us, leave them at baggage claim indefinitely, and strip down to the simple things that make us the happy, whole, authentic us the world needs. Truly us, with just the stuff we can fit into a metaphorical backpack. We need to avoid instant gratification, or paying lip service to change, or excess materialism, or refusing to listen, or second-guessing every situation. We need to keep with us only what is necessary, beloved or beneficial.

Curate your soul and complete a checklist of your mind frequently, to stay aware of your happiness, authenticity – with yourself and those you love – and peace of mind:

- What are your passions? Have you engaged with any of them this week?
- Who do you care about? Have you shown them how you love them this week?
- Where do you feel most calm or most joy? Have you been to any of those places this week, even by allowing yourself to daydream about it, or flicking through old photos, or planning a trip for the future?
- How have you looked after yourself this week? What actions have you taken to build your self-esteem, self-confidence and self-awareness?
- When did you not live authentically this week? If you have any regrets about your actions or interactions, or found yourself comparing yourself to others, think about why you acted this way and what can be learnt to move ahead positively.

Forward planning

The three cornerstones for a life lived with personal authenticity are:

1 Moral integrity Accept your principles and get to grips with your moral code: the habits and traits that make you feel good about yourself, that allow you to sleep well at night or to look in the mirror proudly. Sometimes your values or morals will be unpopular or controversial, and it will seem easier to compromise than to rock the boat, but in the long term, you cannot and should not compromise your character. If something is important to you, it would be inauthentic to pretend that it isn't. You don't have to roar from the rooftops, but hold your morals and beliefs firm in your thoughts and actions.

2 Self-knowledge Be aware of your boundaries, your weaknesses and your strengths. Accepting that you cannot be perfect or brilliant at all pursuits, or be there for all people all the time, or know about all things, is powerful. You have mapped out a realistic plan for your life going forward, a blueprint for where you can realistically achieve more or achieve less, where you can speed up or slow down. You will fail at times, and those failings will help you to show compassion to others, build your own resilience and push you to be less judgemental about yourself and those around you. If everything were too easy, you'd think that life was easy – and it isn't. It is hard for people (and you) in a million different ways, hidden too often under bravado, addictions, social constructs or unkindness.

3 Belief in your individuality: your core values, your future goals, your quirks and foibles. You are all good. You are enough. You don't have to go along with the crowd because the crowd is not walking your unique path. Some people will join you for bits of your walk, then take a left or a right turn, or drop behind or race ahead. That's *their* decision. It's *their* life. The road is long, and the only person who will be with you the whole way is *you*. Don't try to slipstream into another person's journey. Edit, delete, borrow, correct, condense, manage and direct your life with full awareness of your heart and head – not anyone else's.

The blame game

Whenever a shocking news story stops us in our tracks, we feel sad and anxious for a few moments, and we make grand gestures in social media posts about shunning this strange new culture we find ourselves in when followers count more than friends and what's outside counts more than what's inside. We hashtag our socks off, screengrab quotes about empathy to share, and feel part of the solution when we take two seconds to sign a petition. But we need to make kindness and authenticity a priority in real life, too, not just in type. We need to talk the talk, walk the walk, and stop spouting disingenuous twaddle to get more likes. We must cut back on the faux to focus on the real; we must stop saying yes to a culture that values success more than happiness; we must edit our daily lives to include deeper connections with people and places we love and delete the habits we know that don't serve our mental or physical well-being, or the people we love.

We need to own our part in these worrying social trends. We have been refusing to accept the blame for too long now. Every time we complain about social media or the media, we must accept that we *are* social media, and that newspapers, magazines and websites only publish what *we* buy and what *we* want to read. There needs to be a collective change. If you don't like how social media has treated a celebrity, stop engaging with it. Discuss the downsides with your friends face to face instead. If you've been trolled, decide to spend your time on things that nurture you, not make you feel stressed or anxious, and delete your account – even if it's just for a month until you feel stronger or feel you've broken your addiction. And if you don't like a media outlet's message, vote with your purse and stop purchasing it. Look for outlets that feed your soul, help you grow and make you happy. And if you do continue participating, remember that every like or comment you share will affect someone's day. You are judging a human being, not a faceless stranger. Don't be cavalier with your criticisms. Everyone is going through something you know nothing about. Stop shifting blame away. Admit your part in this cultural shift towards the counterfeit and often unthinkingly cruel, and start afresh today. Be kind. And if you can't be kind, keep quiet.

Don't believe the hype

The future could be bringing big things for you – beautiful dreams do come true, and all the trappings of a successful life could continue to flow, or start flowing, your way. This is all brilliant, but heed a warning: beware of the arse-lickers. Let your mum tell you how fabulous, clever and brilliant you are, and it will be nice to hear that from your boss at times, too. But the more you climb your chosen ladder; the more sycophants will start hanging at your ankles trying to lick your boots. Not only is their devotion rarely kosher, but it can also do terrible things to your ego. Getting too high an opinion of yourself will start to add disingenuous layers over the real you – the you your siblings and school friends love.

Ultimately, it doesn't matter how cool, rich or talented you are, how you treat the people around you is the real test of what kind of a person you are. Never let your ego reign so unchecked that you start dismissing other's opinions, ignoring those who knew and loved you before the success set in, and never start to think of yourself as better than anyone else. When I ran *OK!* magazine, and I would dine and party with billionaires and A-listers everywhere from Beverly Hills to Bora Bora, I was horrified to witness how they'd smarm and charm me, then be rude to our waiters or their secretaries. I got their number, and remembered it – and I checked in regularly with my own ego to make sure that I'd never become like that. Treat everyone how you would like to be treated: it really is that simple. As a sign at my favourite Texan restaurant says, 'Be nice to those you pass on your way up as you may meet them on your way down.'

When you don't believe your own hype, you don't have to believe the negativity either. That's the biggest benefit to your mental health. Because for all the sycophants who bend over backwards to worship you, there'll be the trolls who want to pull you down. These are the moments you need to stay centred and authentic, not allowing your self-worth or self-esteem to flip according to someone else's opinion of you. Be clear in your goals, values, strengths and weaknesses, and turn off the noise from the baying crowd. Do you value *you*? That is enough.

Getting real: Abby, 35

'We don't always need more. And, sometimes the person we need to tell no to is ourselves. Question your motives. Are we making work for ourselves? Is this something we really need? Will it bring us joy? Is it necessary? Yes, we want to make birthdays and holidays magical for our children, but they will remember our stress over the time together if we make it a drama. They will not remember that all their birthday packages had bows, or that the Christmas cards went out on time, or that there weren't any dust bunnies under the sofa. Find the ability to say no to some of the items you are adding unnecessarily to the weird list that's dictating to you. Ask yourself questions about what really matters to your family and don't be worried or feel lesser if your answers may sound lazy or unambitious to anyone else.'

Lists for the life you want to lead

Spontaneity and surprises are fun, but when it comes to plotting a fulfilling life story, a list can really help to keep you on track. Note down the key edits you wish to make today, in the next year, in the next decade – the things that will boost your happiness and well-being or get you a much-wanted tick on your bucket list. Sit quietly, contemplate where you are now and where you want to be, focus on the feelings you get in your heart or your tummy when you think about something, then write it down:

- Things I need to apologise for to move on.
- Things I need to forgive or forget to move on. ▶

- Walls I need to tear down to have the space to be free.
- Walls I need to rebuild to find the security that I need to feel safe.
- People I need to let into my heart and allow to know the real me.
- People I need to let go of to heal my heart and become the real me.
- Routines I need to follow to maximise my mental and physical health.
- Rituals I need to practise to maximise my happiness and contentment.

Friends with spiritual benefits

My good friend Anna Humble is a Harvard Divinity scholar, vicar and yoga instructor – a really useful combination to have in a mate who wants you to be happy, even for an agnostic like me. During our many conversations, she has taught me about the salvation that can be found *not* in a god but in a spiritual practice. 'The ancient Hebrews were often derided by other cultures as "lazy" because they dedicated the last day of every week to rest, believing that God had commanded it for them. Sabbath was meant to be a day for reading, gathering with family and community, sharing a holy meal, and even making love. No work was to be done – even non-Jewish servants and labourers were to be given the day off.

'Regardless of whether or not one believes in God or the commandments, the notion of Sabbath was and is still wildly radical – this notion that one should, and even could, dedicate one day each and every week to resting, reading, family, communing, and love-making seems impossible to most people. To hold firm to the ideal of the Sabbath, Jews have repeatedly had to say no for centuries to their surrounding cultures of workaholism, excess, busyness and competition. Even so, the Jewish people have survived and even thrived in the most trying of circumstances despite the fact that they have stepped out of the ring every seventh day.

'Perhaps we can't find a way to take a whole day for Sabbath in our lives, but perhaps we can schedule a Sabbath morning, afternoon, or even an hour. It's a radical idea to opt out of the world for a day, but it's worth a try. As we continue to white-knuckle our way through life, trying to have it all at once, treating ourselves to try to smooth over all the stress, perhaps we should try to swim in the other direction – embracing the Sabbath in order that we might thrive in a very real way that we didn't think was possible before. I followed this example four years ago when I became so plagued by my full-time job and motherhood that I became "Old Yeller". My family would do something irritating, and because of the constant stress buzzing around inside me, which I had come to accept as normal, each small infraction would set me off. I felt immense guilt at my behaviour, so for Lent I decided to give up social media and use that time to read and meditate instead. For 40 evenings in a row, I sat on a meditation pillow, lit tea candles, each representing something I was grateful for, and just sat. I did nothing. I expected nothing.

'One day I realised while folding the laundry that without really trying, without any harsh methods of self-discipline, without any white-knuckled will, my yelling had stopped. I came to understand in these quiet moments that it was time for me to say no to our culture's definition of success as having it all. Perhaps some women I graduated Harvard with were able to do it, be a successful working mother – and certainly many must do it – but I couldn't in those days. For my literal sanity, then, for my family, I had to check my ego, quit my miserably important job, and retire from my martyr complex. Instead, I needed to do normal self-care: to sleep, eat, walk, play. I learnt that self-care isn't about more, it's about less. Our culture will tell you that self-care means "treat yourself" with a spa day, a bottle of rose, or with a little "retail therapy". Let me tell you, I've tried that brand of self-care, and it left me with an empty wallet and with a killer hangover. Safeguarding your time, heart and sense of community is real self-care.'

Safeguarding, supplementing and saying no

As Anna's study tells us, some of us have knowingly been cutting back, accepting things as they are and saying no for centuries, understanding that is where peace of mind and deep connection – and therefore happiness – comes from. It's still so tempting to hit the world at full speed, though, isn't it, because to be left out would mean that we are unpopular or not success-ful enough. We need a conscious movement of thought around this, a shift in society, because when depression, anxiety and suicide rates are increasing – despite everyone looking so perfect on Instagram – we know we need to address our constant need for more, more, more and must, must, must.

- Treasure your cornerstones – the things that keep you grounded and sane.

- Authenticity is about staying true to your thoughts, feelings and beliefs, it is not about image. It is about matching what we feel inside with what we show to the world on the outside. Of course, looking good is important to our self-esteem and can put a spring in our step, but it is when our inner beauty matches our outside that we are truly stunning. As Roald Dahl wrote, 'A person who has good thoughts cannot ever be ugly. You can have a wonky nose and a crooked mouth and a double chin and stick-out teeth, but if you have good thoughts they will shine out of your face like sunbeams and you will always look lovely.'

- Lying is stressful, so stick to minimal white lies only to help others and protect their feelings. Big lies (like the ones sought out with lie detector tests, which measure the off-putting physical symptoms of lying such as erratic breathing and a quickening heart rate) are stressful for our mind and body; however, living in your truth does not mean having to share every truth that you've discovered. Sometimes it's a good idea to keep things to yourself. Follow the rule I teach my children, 'If you can't say anything nice, don't say anything at all.'

- Feel what is real – physically. Your body will respond to actions or words that are inauthentic. Your stomach will churn, your muscles will spasm, your head will ache. When you live in truth, you live lighter and brighter.

- Own your ugly. Show yourself compassion and forgiveness, and share your weaknesses with those who love you. If we present a curated, ideal image to the world, we will not allow connection on a meaningful level with our own soul or others. The more we own our foibles, the more others will feel able to share, talk, find solutions and not feel so alone.

Perform a 'life scan'

For a few years, a fellow parent I knew loosely from classroom parties and school concerts had intrigued me greatly. When we were first aware of each other, when our boys joined the reception year together, she was – in my eyes – a bit of a busybody and a chatterbox. I liked her vibe, it was friendly and witty, but it always felt a little pulled, distracted and rushed, and I felt that she was always looking over her shoulder to see if someone with more social currency was approaching. But in the last 12 months, she'd noticeably calmed. Having zero fucks to give and always looking to learn, I complimented her on her new demeanour and asked her what had happened.

She'd done 'a life scan' – yes, she'd placed everything down in front of her and scanned it like a photocopier. 'At 43, I began scanning my life and making the necessary edits,' she said. 'I soon got on a roll, limiting my expectations, living in the present moment and weaning myself off Facebook. Next up is my boundaries. I am what is called a functioning co-dependent. I want everyone to be happy, so saying no is extremely hard for me, but I know I have to start. This year I'm working on saying no to things that I really do not want to do to make way for opportunities for things that I do want to do.'

She'd bought a paper calendar and decided to start with writing her work/family commitments down. The number of calendar squares that were filled in was jarring. 'Every single day, I had work, kids, volunteering and social commitments – and the list went on. I knew my life was busy but seeing it on paper was eye-opening. I had to create some boundaries; I had to protect my time much better.' My friend built in buffer zones of nothing. 'I try not to leave the house for more than two nights a week. I cleared up my calendar and made sure that there were as many blank spaces as possible. Now, instead of always saying yes and running all over the place like a chicken with my head cut off, I am mindful of my yeses. I make sure that my time is protected. Along the lines of implementing boundaries, I make sure my children's time is also protected. I don't allow many weekly after-school playdates, I am mindful of their time and if they happen to have a busy day, I always make sure to schedule buffer zones in between activities. And sometimes that means they miss out on something, and that's OK.'

Setting boundaries and saying no had literally turned the woman from distracted to delightful ... and I stole her idea of building buffer zones into my family's busy schedule.

Journal your journey – your life scan

If you were to perform your own life scan, what five things would you buffer or build? What five hopes to hold for the future, after completing this life edit? Make a list and jot down how and when you can make them happen. Revisit the list frequently to check in on your progress. Feel free to add things as they come up or to cross things off when they are no longer relevant.

Annual antagoniser

You can be living your happiest, most authentic life and then – slap, bang, wallop – here comes the anniversary of another trip around the sun. Birthdays can be tough – yes, you're another year older, and wiser (let's hope) – but there can also be a sense of pressure to party, or the dread of getting older and, maybe, physically less perfect. A big help in getting a grip can be owning your age. I heard my mother-in-law explain her forehead wrinkles away to my six-year-old daughter recently as 'a line for everyone I love' – marks accumulated over time, showing on her face the love she feels in her heart. I feel this way about my ageing, post-baby body. The stretch marks are mama warrior symbols – I grew, I birthed, I adored. I may be saggier on the outside, but inside I possess the heart of a lion. Look at birthdays as a chance to show gratitude and reflect. As I say when friends moan and groan about hitting another birthday or spotting a new wrinkle, 'the alternative is much worse'. Feel lucky for every extra year.

Ding, dong, merrily on high-stress

It is the best of times; it is the worst of times. I'm talking about the festive madness of December, of course. I love the glittery streets, jingly bells and marshmallow world as much as your next overgrown child, but there is something so sad about the frenetic, overloaded and expensive way we have recreated this celebration. 'Tis the season to be broke, stressed, tired and competitive, it seems. It is at this point, more than ever, that we need to hang on to our focus on quality over quantity and accepting our limits that we've built into our lives during the rest of the year. Because Christmas after Christmas I am devastated to see women who are normally calm and rational lose the plot – unable to sleep, anxious about getting 'it all' done, worried about money, about finding the perfect gift for a cousin they don't even like. And for what? For whom?

'It's for my children!' the mothers gasp from under a pile of Amazon boxes and tinsel, but we know the children (and your bank balance) will be fine with a couple of thoughtfully chosen gifts, meaningful time with family and friends and some quirky treats such as waking to chocolate advent calendars, or pyjama screenings of *Elf* past their normal bedtimes. Because it is scary, but true, that the average child in the developed world owns over 200 toys but plays with only 12 of them on an average day. When it comes to kids' bedrooms, less is certainly more. My children can feel overwhelmed by choice and bury things. When we have a charity shop clear-out, they value each item more if they have carefully considered and decided to keep it, and they actually play with everything they have once their bedrooms are free from excess clutter.

'It's for my parents,' the daughters sigh, while fighting off a cold and fighting to get the last box of After Eights at their local supermarket ... without understanding that their parents hate seeing their baby breaking at the seams under the weight of ridiculous standards and expectations, and are just happy that they are no longer the ones who have to get up at 3am to stuff the turkey and creep around the house, cringing at every floorboard creek, filling stockings full of plastic toot.

No, the truth is that we've brought this festive frenzy of overspending and showing off on ourselves. When I used to hear acquaintances declare 'I've got 12 parties per day from now until January 2nd' I used to feel an unrecognisable surge of envy that all this fun was going on without me. *How come I've only got two Christmas trips to the theatre, one film outing, one work party, and three girls' lunches?* I'd inwardly groan, feeling the weight of unpopularity and FOMO. Now, having worked hard to find balance and know my limits. and respecting my inner introvert, I feel genuine sympathy. *They must feel so worn down*, my inner old lady thinks, feeling grateful that I'll be spending most evenings with two friends who demand little of me, Ferrero and Rocher, in a quiet little town called Schitt's Creek.

Five reasons to say no, no, no to excessive ho-ho-ho

1. Toasting the season is fun, but overdoing the alcohol will leave you dehydrated, exhausted and possibly racked with that bizarre post-booze guilt that so many of us get in adulthood. Too much eggnog will also weaken your immune system – so own your Shirley Temple mocktail or hot chocolate days.

2. You've worked out what food and fitness routines work for your mental and physical health. Don't throw it all away in the run-up to Christmas assuming you'll be saint-like from 1 January. A 2018 study by the University of Scranton shows that

80 per cent of people fail to keep their New Year's resolutions, another study stating that most people have given up on their goals by 12 January. Indulge in what feels festive and good to you, but don't be pressured into going all out for things you could easily say no to.

3. Be mindful of what makes you feel festive and warm, not what others tell you should. If you want to have mini discos at home, dancing to Shakin' Stevens's 'Merry Christmas Everyone' on repeat because it reminds you of your grandma, rather than accepting every invitation to a 'glam and glitter' night out, so be it.

4. Don't fall into the overly jolly trap of pretending that everything is OK and shiny if it isn't. Make sure you connect with people on authentic levels. Check in with friends who might be lonely, do something kind for the friend who has lost someone they love that year and look for ways to support your community. Not everyone is wearing an ugly sequinned Christmas jumper and heading to a karaoke bar.

5. Remember that it is only one day. Don't become the festive version of a bridezilla, building these few hours up into a stress-zone fuelled with worry and ego. Plan things for January so that you have things to look forward to – and, no, I don't mean a cabbage soup diet plan, I mean concerts and plays, weekends away, or an evening with friends.

Happy hibernation

I'm an avid advocate of clearing your personal path of the unnecessary and unhealthy, and finding your own route to calm,
centred contentment – and never is this more needed or apparent
than during the colder months. There is a reason why the trees
give up their energetic bounty to autumn, and spend winter still
and bare, and animals curl up to recuperate for their next burst
of growing in the forthcoming spring. Hibernating is something
that we could all do a bit more of. Follow the sun and rest when
she does. Spend a day in your pyjamas without feeling guilty – use
the time indoors to finish the niggling jobs you've been putting
off all year, to start the next one with a clean slate. Stock up on
the small pleasures you don't seem to allot time to in the warmer,
brighter months: a pile of books by your bed to while away an
afternoon, baking childhood fancies, napping with abandon,
movie marathons. Reject invitations that you know you'll later
regret accepting. It's OK to admit that you have too much on and
schedule alone time in your diary – or family at home time at
least. You've decorated your tree, but have you poured yourself a
cuppa and allowed yourself to drift off in its glow, reminiscing
about past Christmases and the memories you have? Probably not.

Getting real: Jessica, 35

'For the last few years, December was my toughest
month, which saddened me because as a child – with
a December birthday *and* Christmas – it was magical.
As a mum, I felt I was always rushing with little time to

actually reflect on the year that had whizzed by, fighting against a huge imaginary clock I'd set myself, while getting dragged into small talk at never-ending social events and comparing myself to other people and their prettier festive season on Instagram. It was my ten-year-old who actually made me chill out and omit the unnecessary from our calendar. 'Why are you trying to please everyone else when you always tell me to be kind but to know what makes me feel happy and healthy?' he asked. I told him I didn't know – guilt, expectations, the desire to be perfect. He tutted in the way that only pre-teens can. On Christmas Day, I found a hand-drawn voucher from him under the tree for "mum alone time" – and I used it!'

The gift of life

Presents are fun, but whether it's for a thank you or birthday gift, or at Christmas, Hanukkah or at a wedding, research shows that experiences can be more rewarding and have longer-lasting positive feelings associated with them than material goods. In a survey by LinkedIn, 73 per cent of workers said they'd rather experience something fun or cool with a loved one than receive a gift or a monetary bonus. And just think of the waste! Recent data indicates that Americans spend over $15 billion on unwanted gifts that will sit getting dusty in the back of a closet for all eternity. Another scary statistic: storage facilities are the fastest growing area for building and renting in the US, with the UK not far behind, and one in ten of us now have to use a storage unit to store our excess things.

We all have too much stuff, too much clutter – and it's costing us dearly, financially and mentally. Meanwhile, research by Cornell University highlights that while pleasure derived from material goods generally fades quickly, the feel-good release from shared experiences and adventures lasts a long time, which is especially beneficial to children. Shared experiences help them bond with friends and family and give them a strong sense of security and identity. And think how much neater their bedrooms will be without all that plastic and packaging? Focus on what your family and friends really need, not on creating the perfect image of your tree groaning and glittering with perfectly wrapped presents.

Ideas to make memories, not mess

- Design 'coupons' for a unique service that you can donate: babysitting, watering plants or caring for a pet while they take a holiday, or giving them a pedicure.
- Give a wellness experience you can share: take them to a salt cave, join them on a forest walk with a picnic, buy them a class pass to the local yoga studio and allot time in your schedules to practise together.
- Send them to a restaurant or bar where you have a special menu or bottle of wine ready for them and paid for.
- Purchase advance tickets for an upcoming movie, concert or exhibition.

- Craft something unique: make a photo book, knit a scarf, build a small indoor herb garden.
- Sign up for memberships to local galleries, gardens or museums for year-long fun.
- Get the equipment needed for a fun getaway: tents, sleeping bags and a s'mores kit for sunset marshmallow roasting on a campsite, or swimsuits and snorkelling gear for a beach adventure.
- Choose a charity you know is special to your recipient and make a donation in their name.
- Learn a new skill together: pay for pottery classes, horseback riding, life painting, and so on.
- Download a newspaper or magazine subscription on to their device, or fill their Kindle with some much-loved or much-desired books and albums.

Getting real: Stephanie, 43

'Learning how to say no has everything to do with value. We say yes for one of many reasons including, but not limited to: it will make my kids happy; it will make me feel appreciated, it has to get done, no one else will do it. But none of those reasons include: it's good for me. We assign so much value to how our actions might be appreciated by others that we forget to acknowledge if we really care about any of it. I learnt to say no when I saw that my kids didn't care about superfluous things. They cared that I was there to give them a hug after school when a kid had been mean, and that I was listening when they were telling me a long-winded story about the science project that fell apart. They just wanted me there. All of me. So that is what I strive for now. To sit next to them on the couch when there's a television show on that they love. To remember that a boy was at lunch that had caught my teenager's eye. To tell them when I'm tired and accept a hug to make me feel better too. None of that is on Pinterest, but it's so much less stressful.'

Own your story – here's how

As you look towards the future, and imagine your most authentic, happy life, use this check in to imprint, correct and remember the key points of your true personality, and the supplements or withdrawals you require to maintain it.

Ace your apology game

Clear up your mental debris by confronting your past hurts and mistakes, saying sorry – to others and your sensitive self – and sitting with your lessons.

Upgrade your habits

What traits could you acquire for a healthier life? A wise friend recently told me that she'd started 'living without pretending, loving without depending, listening without defending and speaking without offending' – and I thought: *Dang it, girl, that's the source of all goodness right there!* We need those life lessons printed on a T-shirt, am I correct?

Treat yourself kindly

Are you keeping busy or putting on a show to stay numb, to forget, to try to be popular, to impress someone? You can't do this for ever. You have to take the mask off at night, and when you are left with yourself you need to be OK. The main person I want you to impress is yourself: the you who has seen you struggle, heard your cries, held your hand, felt your trauma. The you who has the power to avoid a burnout or a breakdown. Sit silently with yourself. Be proud that you still exist. Be proud of what you've overcome. Be real in your quest to be honest, healthy and happy. Don't get distracted by the glitter or noise.

Humility is a must-have

Accept who you are with modesty and a humble approach to your achievements. It'll be harder to knock you off the rollercoaster of life with a practical, centred, realistic view of yourself, with an ego in check. Take care with other people's feelings, and your own.

Enjoy your assets

Our society has us counting calories, money, kilos, steps and promotions while we should be counting our blessings and strengths. We all have something to be grateful for.

▶

N arrow down negativity

Get picky about who and what you allow into your life. As you rebuild, only allow things into your inner sanctum that bring peace, joy and good health. To the negative stuff, be polite but be strong – say no, admit that it won't work for you, own your discomfort, ask for a pause. Every brick of your fortress should count for something or someone worthwhile. A few years ago, when I was continuously stressed out about a mean-spirited friend, an aunt said to me, 'Don't blame the clown for acting like a clown, blame yourself for still buying tickets to her circus!' You *must* take charge of who you allow into your life.

T rue colours make your rainbow – the shiniest, most vibrant version of you. Remember, it's more important to be yourself than to be popular. If you think that no one will like you if you share your true colours, know that you are either (a) wrong; or (b) hanging with the wrong people. True friends enjoy true colours – the pot of gold for us all is getting an authentic, happy friend who expresses, shares and loves with all they have. Be so completely yourself that everyone around you feels safe to be them-selves, as well.

'I don't' . . .

Create a list of deal breakers, mind clutterers, energy suck-ers and good-vibe fuckers that you refuse to engage with. Lists are not just for remembering what you *do* need; they can also remind you what you *don't* need, too.

Cut to the chase

This is your only go at this. Make it count. Tell your story. Stop saying yes, stop apologising for being you, cut back on the clutter, flick away the phoney and work out your real deal. Commit to your values, your self-care, your body and your brain. Get specific about how you want to be treated and keep your boundaries. Be authentic.

Epilogue

'She was becoming herself and daily casting aside that fictitious self which we assume like a garment with which to appear before the world.'

Kate Chopin, *The Awakening*

A few weeks ago, in an antiques shop, I saw a funny ashtray with an inscription on it: 'As soon as the rush is over, I'm going to have the nervous breakdown I deserve. I owe it to myself, I worked for it, and nobody is going to deprive me of it.' Despite it being made in the 1960s, the sentiment on the glass seemed to be a philosophy that many people around me still subscribe to today. Perhaps more so than when this ashtray was made 50 years ago.

What I've learnt over my decade of self-editing is that we don't have to rush, shout or search for drama or praise until breaking point. We are not a movie about Wall Street. We are human. We can be silent, hold our space, hold our bodies and mind protectively, and hold our tender moments close to us. We don't need to cram every second, every moment, every corner, every space in our diary, brain or home. Just *being* is perfectly acceptable.

As a work in progress, we are never done. In a way that tourists should never proclaim that they have 'done India' or 'done Athens', you as the holidaymaker in your own head and heart, can never be *done* with yourself. You must edit thoughtfully, frequently and judiciously. You must check in with every character you've written on your pages, make sure that every location is working for your story, and think about every plotline and where the twists and turns are taking you. You shouldn't end up reading your life back knowing that it could have been better, sweeter, calmer or clearer when you know you had the tools to make it so.

You can never ignore your triggers, for they can pop and bang, then ricochet around your psyche without any warning. I know this too well. Writing *Get Real* broke me before it could rebuild me, I'll be honest. As I researched, and reviewed my life, and engaged in conversations with people I love about their difficult journeys towards authenticity – while the news from around the world felt so desperately sad and anxious – I felt vulnerable and raw, and I re-questioned everything. I'd dream of people from my past, waking sweaty at 3am wracked with guilt, or a heaviness that kept me awake till sunrise, reimagining final conversations, the things I wish I'd said. I'd suddenly recall a hurtful comment from nowhere – a constant joke about my size I'd endured when I was a teen; a flashback to a fight with a colleague; a bitchy comment from a supposed friend that had made its way back to me. Ghosts and demons showed up uninvited at the most unexpected, loveliest moments. Ultimately it was helpful. Because being open, real and owning your shit is the only way you can move forward, and work out what works for you.

The world doesn't need any more fake BS. We have enough

of that from our media, politicians, nemeses and buried inner demons. What we need now is all our legit, deep, credible, genuine, tangible pain; we need it out there, worked through, listened to, reflected upon and let go of. The false, implausible, unequal and invalid structures that we've built our lives upon, individually and collectively, are going to crumble at some point – or multiple points – so by taking charge, using our strengths and accepting our weaknesses, by editing in our own time and style, we can move forward to an authentic life we love. We need to stop saying 'be kind', 'chill out', 'be real'. We need to start *living* kindness, calm and truth. You don't need to write about it on Instagram; you need to just *do* it.

This morning, before I sat down to write this final paragraph, I went to my first hot-yoga class. The instructor asked us to dedicate our hour to something, and I chose to focus on accepting my imperfections. As I stretched myself, all creaking, clicking joints and sweat beads, I was able to ignore the more limber, bendy creatures on the mats around me, and get lost in my own abilities, needs and limits. The instructor kept repeating softly, 'Your choices, your practice; your options, your practice.' I listened and readjusted myself, I worked a bit harder at some moments, then let myself slide in others, forehead to the mat when I needed to slow down. I thought how her mantra could help us to see every aspect of our lives more clearly. It was a reminder that this life is there for the taking – and there for the breaking. Your life is your practice, but of course, we don't get a practice run. This is it.

As Toni Morrison wrote, 'you wanna fly, you got to give up the shit that weighs you down'. The expectations, the energy suckers, the fraudsters, the rigmaroles built around perfection and social pressure – that is the shit. Embracing your ability to say no, cut back, be kind and editing your way into an authentic, happy life will make you feel so much lighter.

Drop the dead weight. Embrace your strengths. Accept your limits. Head up high to an ever-changing sky and don't look down, just trust yourself. Then fly, baby, fly.

Sources

References

For more on the research included in and inspiring *Get Real*:

Akers, A., J. Barton, et al., 'Visual color perception in green exercise: Positive effects on mood and perceived exertion', *Environmental Science and Technology*, 46(16):8661–6 (2012), print

Alden, L.E. and J.L. Trew, 'Kindness reduces avoidance goals in socially anxious individuals', *Motivation and Emotion*, 39(6): 892 (2015), print

Armenta, Christina N., et al. 'Functions of positive emotions: Gratitude as a motivator of self-improvement and positive change', *Emotion Review*, 9(3):183–90 (2017), print

Aspinall, P., P. Mavros, et al., 'The urban brain: Analyzing outdoor physical activity with mobile EEG', *British Journal of Sports Medicine*, (2012), print

Barr, S., 'The average Brit checks their phone 10,000 times a year, study finds', Independent.co.uk, 1 December 2017, Web

Barton, J. and J. Pretty 'What is the best dose of nature and green exercise for improving mental health? A multi-study analysis', *Environmental Science and Technology*, 44:3947–55 (2010), print

Berman, M.G., J. Jonides, S. Kaplan, 'The cognitive benefits of interacting with nature', *Psychological Science*, 19:1207–12 (2008), print

Bolderdijk, J.W. and Y. Joye, 'An exploratory study into the effects of extraordinary nature on emotions, mood, and prosociality', *Frontiers in Psychology* 5:1577 (2015), print

Chadborn, D., and S. Reysen, 'Moved by the masses: A social identity perspective on inspiration', *Current Psychology: A Journal for Diverse Perspectives on Diverse Psychological Issues*, (2016), print

Dunbar, R.I.M., 'Do online social media cut through the constraints that limit the size of offline social networks?', *Royal Society Open Science*, 1 January 2016, Web

Ghent, A. 'The happiness effect', *Bulletin of the World Health Organization*, 4 April 2011, Web

Glass, J., R.W. Simon and M.A. Andersson, 'The parenthood "happiness penalty": The effects of social policies in 22 countries', *PRC Research Brief*, 2(7) (2016), print

Helliwell, J., R. Layard, and J. Sachs, *Journal of World Happiness Report*, 2019, New York: Sustainable Development Solutions Network, Web

Holt-Lunstad, J., T.B. Smith and J.B. Layton, 'Social relationships and mortality risk: A meta-analytic review', *PLoS Med*, 7(7) (2010), print

Hone, L.C., A. Jarden, G.M. Schofield, and S. Duncan, 'Measuring flourishing: The impact of operational definitions on the prevalence of high levels of wellbeing', *International Journal of Wellbeing*, 4(1):62–90, (2014), print

Huang, Ru-Yi, et al., 'Vegetarian diets and weight reduction: a Meta-analysis of randomized controlled trials', *Journal of General Internal Medicine* 31(1):109–16 (2016), print

Johnston, W.M. and G.C.L. Davey, 'The psychological impact of negative TV news bulletins: The catastrophizing of personal worries', *British Journal of Psychology*, 88: 85–91 (1997), print

Kalmback, David A., P. Vivek, et al., 'The interplay between daily affect and sleep: A 2-week study of young women', *Journal of Sleep Research*, 23(6) (2014), print

Kelly, A.E., 'Lying less linked to better health', *American Psychological Association*, 4 August 2012, Web

Lee, J., B.-J. Park, et al., 'Restorative effects of viewing real forest landscapes, based on a comparison with urban landscapes', *Scandinavian Journal of Forest Research*, 24(3):227–34 (2009), print

Park, B.-J., K. Furuya, et al., 'Relationship between psychological responses and physical environments in forest settings', *Landscape and Urban Planning*, 102(1):24–32 (2011), print

Park, B.-J., Y. Tsunetsugu, et al., 'The physiological effects of Shinrin-yoku (taking in the forest atmosphere or forest bathing): Evidence from field experiments in 24 forests across Japan', *Environmental Health and Preventative Medicine*, 15(1):18–26 (2010), print

Prathik K., J. Wong, et al., 'The effects of gratitude expression on neural activity', *NeuroImage Journal*, (2016), print

Pruthi, S., et al., 'Friendships: Enrich your life and improve your health', Mayoclinic.org, 28 September 2016, Web

Scheier, M. F., C. Wrosch, et al., 'The Life Engagement Test: Assessing purpose in life', *Journal of Behavioral Medicine*, 29(3):291 (2006)

Tromholt, M., 'The Facebook experiment: Quitting Facebook leads to higher levels of well-being', *Cyberpsychology, Behaviour, and Social Networking*, 19(11) (2016), print

Tsunetsugu, Y., L. Lee, et al., 'Physiological and psychological effects of viewing urban forest landscapes assessed by multiple measurements', *Landscape and Urban Planning*, 113:90–93 (2013), print

Ulrich, R.S., 'Effects of gardens on health outcomes: Theory and research', in C. Cooper-Marcus and M. Barnes (eds), *Healing Gardens: Therapeutic Benefits and Design Recommendations*, New York: John Wiley, pp. 27–86 (1999), print

Utley, T., '7,994 hours of our lives spent in regret? Not I – even though I missed a chance to be a millionaire', *Daily Mail*, 11 February 2020, print

Zamani S., and S. Hojjat, et al., 'Physical activity and self-esteem: Testing direct and indirect relationships associated with psychological and physical mechanisms', *Neuropsychiatric Disease and Treatment*, 12:2617–25 (2016), print

Useful websites

European Social Survey: europeansocialsurvey.org

Headstogether.org.uk

Mentalhealth.org.uk

Mind.org.uk

New Economics Foundation: nationalaccountsofwellbeing.org

Stressmanagement.org

Well-being in Gallup surveys: gallup.com/topic/category_
   wellbeing.aspx

Well-being in the UK: ons.gov.uk/
   peoplepopulationandcommunity/wellbeing

World Health Organization: who.int

About the Author

Sarah Ivens, PhD, is the best-selling author of ten lifestyle and wellness books, including *A Modern Girl's Guide to Getting Hitched* and *Forest Therapy: Seasonal Ways to Embrace Nature for a Happier You*, and the founding editor-in-chief of *OK!* magazine in the US.

A Londoner, she now lives in Austin, Texas, after five years in New York, where she ran *OK!* and two years in Los Angeles, where she worked for the drama development team at HBO and certified as a life coach.

Sarah holds a PhD in Comparative Humanities from the University of Louisville, Kentucky, her work focusing on the changes and choices faced by women during the reign of Elizabeth II, and how the ideas of home and homeland shape a woman's life. She is a contributor to the *Daily Mail*, the *Telegraph*, *Stella*, *Glamour*, *Marie Claire*, the *New York Post* and *YOU* magazine, among others.

Sarah's other books include *A Modern Girl's Guide to Dynamic Dating*, *A Modern Girl's Guide to Etiquette*, *A Modern Girl's Guide to Getting Hitched*, *A Modern Girl's Guide to the Perfect Single Life*, *A Modern Girl's Guide to Getting Organized*, *A Modern Girl's Guide to Networking*, *Forest Therapy: Seasonal Ways to Embrace Nature for a Happier You*, *The Bride's Guide to Unique Weddings* and *The Zen Mama*, all published by Piatkus. *No Regrets: 101 Fabulous Things to Do Before You're Too Old, Married or Pregnant* is published by Random House. She is also the editor of *Mother, Other: Words by Women on Bereavement*, published by Sarabande Books.